Changing Culture, Changing Care

S.E.R.V.I.C.E FIRST

Susan D. Gilster, Ph.D.

Cincinnati Book Publishing
Jarndyce & Jarndyce Press
www.cincybooks.com

Changing Culture, Changing Care

S.E.R.V.I.C.E FIRST

Susan D. Gilster, Ph.D.

Cover design: Eberhard + Eberhard
Logo design: Christine Mulvin

Published by Cincinnati Book Publishing / Jarndyce & Jarndyce Press
Cincinnati Book Publishers World Wide Web address is
www.cincybooks.com

ISBN: 0-9721916-5-8

Printed by John S. Swift Co., Inc.
Printed in the United States of America
First Edition, November 2005

Comments

"Susan Gilster is a thoughtful leader who has demonstrated the value of culture change in long-term care through her accomplishments. The Service-Oriented Leadership Model encompasses key leadership characteristics and practices needed to develop a service-oriented organizational culture. It is a practical tool that will help long-term care leaders with their culture change efforts. This approach embodies person-centered principles that are essential for improving quality of care and quality of life for all those who are served."

> **Diane L. Dixon,** Ed.D. Managing Principal, D. Dixon & Associates, LLC; Contributing Writer-*Caring for the Ages;* Faculty Practitioner, Business of Medicine-Johns Hopkins University

Susan Gilster's S.E.R.V.I.C.E. model is a must read for those who wish to hone their leadership skills. The book is an absolute gem for beginning and established leaders. This smart, honest, effective, humanistic, down-to-earth model may serve as a balm for leadership in an industry that is in a state of painful flux. Susan is a savvy leader who navigates us through the maze of human relations, recognizing that truly effective leaders must meet basic human needs and lead by serving those they would have follow them. What a powerful concept!

> **Dr. Evelyn L. Fitzwater**
> Associate Professor Nursing
> University of Cincinnati
> Independent Nursing and Health Care Consultant

"This ambitious book is a timely, innovative and invaluable resource for all leaders in the long term care community. In a time when many are seeking answers about how to go about transforming the culture of long-term care, Dr. Gilster provides solid practical advice within an easy to understand theoretical framework distilled from years of experience and a thoughtful translation of the scholarly literature. This well-written book is a "must read" for every person in a leadership position interested in creating a culture of dignity, respect and compassionate care. "

> **Kimberly S. Van Haitsma,** Ph.D.
> Senior Research Scientist
> Polisher Research Institute
> Madlyn & Leonard Abramson Center for Jewish Life

The approaches that long-term care leaders employ over the next 10 years will shape the future of aging services in our country. Research continues to demonstrate that facility leadership shows a relationship with every measure of quality. Dr. Gilster has lived in this world and shares her experiences and the importance of the S.E.R.V.I.C.E. model of leadership with the reader. For those embarking on transformational change – for those knowing that Person-Directed Care is essential – for those wanting to learn about leadership – for everyone involved in Long-Term Care, this book is an essential part of your professional curriculum.

> **Mary Tellis-Nayak,** MSN, MPH
> Business Development Executive
> CARF-CCAC
> Past President and CEO of the American College of Health Care
> Administrators

Dr. Gilster has been a pioneer as a woman and a healthcare professional in building a new model for effective leadership. In the 21st century healthcare and many other industries must blend the new realties of business survival, quality patient care and a workforce that is searching to find meaning in their life and their work. This breakthrough vision is a guide for moving your organization and your team to the highest levels of success.

> **Vanessa Freytag,** Publisher, Women's Business Cincinnati and
> President of W-Insight, Inc.

In her book, Susan Gilster has captured the essence and importance of directed and mentored leadership, it illustrates ways to captivate, enrich and empower the staff through education, coaching and a solid vision.

> **Mark Wellinghoff,** M.S., LNHA
> Carespring Management Resources
> Vice President of Operations

Susan Gilster epitomizes leadership in service. Endowed with vision, energy, and an ethical imperative to meet a societal goal, her gift of soft-spoken, calm, strong leadership demonstrates how a faith in colleagues, under girded by continuing education and exposure to other experts in the field for all under her professional umbrella, can lead to a restoration of human dignity in a mental health environment so often characterized by a paucity of same. Dr. Gilster exudes the confident and optimistic realism that has driven her S.E.R.V.I.C.E. model through the 1987 establishment of her organization—the first of its kind, and in the minds of many researchers, still the best. Quiet, firm, resolved leadership follows this author around—be it in the Cincinnati services sector, the broader national dementia community, or in her private/personal endeavors. No interested reader can get through this text without learning from her leadership model.

Peter Fenner, PhD
Founding Partner, Compass Group, Inc.
Healthcare Consultants since 1979

"Susan dares to listen to new approaches, dares to dream what no one's ever tried, and she succeeds because she approaches the challenges of today's health-care system with a unique combination of her ears, her brain and her heart."

Sue MacDonald, freelance writer and Alzheimer's caregiver

"Susan Gilster is one of the savviest leaders I know. Her academic expertise, real world experience, and innate understanding of how to bring out the best in people is a potent combination. Everyone may not be as naturally talented as Susan is, but anyone can become a more effective leader by following her model of simple and obvious organizational strategies."

Helen B. Habbert
QRC Associates

Dr. Gilster not only has years of experience developing and operating one of the most successful dementia care settings in the U.S.A., she has rigorously studied the practices of other successful leaders. She demonstrates remarkable skill in translating her knowledge and insights into practical information for others, enabling more people to understand what it takes to become a successful leader.

Margaret P. Calkins, M.Arch., Ph.D.

Dr. Susan Gilster is a leader in the field of care for dementia. She has mentored both informal and formal caregivers in providing the environmental milieu that fosters maximal functional capacity. Her coaching methods have spawned an interest in others to adopt a leadership role in caring for frail older adults.

Sally L. Brooks, M.D., FACP, AGS-F

Leadership in health care quality has been a recent topic of concern. Unlike "widget" production, human health care quality cannot be mandated. For nearly 20 years as the CEO of a long term care facility, working with persons with cognitive impairment and their families, Susan wrote daily reflections on what she learned. She used what she learned to continually improve the lives of staff, residents, and families. Hundreds of people, including international visitors visit the Center to learn about the care that Susan has orchestrated. Lucky for all of us, Susan has compiled her approach in a step-by step leadership guide that will transform staff and residential care into a place where you wouldn't mind living yourself.

Ann McCracken, PhD
Former Professor of Nursing, Fulbright teacher/researcher in Norway and Australia, and current Director of Evaluation at a health foundation.

TABLE OF CONTENTS

DEDICATION

This book is dedicated to my husband John, my beloved and best friend; the other two people I cherish most in life, my son Joe and daughter Stephanie; and all of the people of the Alois Alzheimer Center who, through the years, have become my cherished family, too.

ACKNOWLEDGEMENTS

One does not get to this point in life, an opportunity to share one's life work with others, without the help and support of many family members, friends, teachers and colleagues.

I am grateful to my husband, John Gilster for his patience, his willingness to listen and his steadfast belief in me. To my children Joseph and Stephanie, who encourage me and offer me valuable perspectives on life and living. They have supported me with their love and remind me daily of the truly important things in life.

I express my love for my sister, Mary Beth Hunt and brother, Leslie Hunt who remain here on earth - together we share wonderful memories and lots of laughter. For those we have lost, I thank my mother Nancy Hunt, who taught me persistence and convinced me through her actions that there was nothing that I could not accomplish if I was truly committed. Blessed am I for my father, Leslie Hunt, who taught me to think with my heart as well as my head; and my brother Michael Hunt, who taught us about acceptance and unconditional love.

Much of the S.E.R.V.I.C.E. model discussed in this book was utilized and tested in the development and operation of the Alois Alzheimer Center. It would never have come to fruition without the insight of owners Steve Boymel and Henry Schneider. I appreciate their willingness to allow the Alois Alzheimer Center staff to go where no one else had traveled and to trust us to do it well.

I am thankful for an incredible group of individuals who came together around a dream and continue to make dreams come true. They are my colleagues and friends at the Alois Alzheimer Center. Very special thanks to Jennifer Dalessandro for her humor, willingness to listen and steadfast support, Marvin Knobloch for his unselfish, healing spirit, Michelle Huber for her dedication and quality care, Tom Vaughn for his expertise and willingness to help, Ann McCracken for her creativity and free spirit, and Kristen Langhout for her talent and insight. I am truly grateful for the many colleagues who continue to offer their hands and hearts every day to the older adults for whom they care. While I cannot name them all they are clear in my mind, embedded in my memory and forever engraved in my heart.

Fortunately, I also have good friends who make me take time to renew and refresh. Clare Logan, Dr. Sally Brooks, Dr. Evelyn Fitzwater and Mary Waters fill me when I am empty and allow me to be myself completely. Together we have shared many crazy moments, boat rides and beautiful sunsets at our get-away haven in Hope Town, Bahamas.

Many individuals have touched my life and made significant contributions, from the young man who taught me all he could about life before he died, to the old man with the red shirts. They have been an inspiration to me, providing lessons in courage, kindness and unconditional love.

PROLOGUE

Frank

Frank is a 210-pound man with a diagnosis of Alzheimer's disease. He lives in a long-term care facility. Today Frank is visibly upset. He is pacing through the unit, looking for something that he cannot describe in words. He paces faster and faster, tearing linens off the beds and going through dresser drawers in one room after another. A staff member grabs his arm from behind as he rips a sheet from another bed. He pulls his arm away and looks as if he might strike her. She screams for help. Frank is startled by the scream. He pushes his way out through the doorway, only to see a crowd of staff descend upon him. Six staff members wrestle him to the floor, holding him down while the nurse gives him yet another injection. He fights with all of his might, frightened and panicked.

George

George is a new resident in a nursing facility. He is a large man, with a diagnosis of dementia. George is restless today, wandering all over the unit. He looks worried, afraid, and moves from space to space with increasing anxiety. Pam, a certified nursing assistant, approaches him, speaking quietly. He stops. She stands in front of him and looks into his eyes, quietly humming a song. She smiles and waits, and when it is time, she gently takes his hands, one by one. Still looking into his eyes, she hums and smiles. As she starts to sway from side to side, George moves with her. Still humming, she leads him in a slow and gentle dance. He smiles, no longer anxious, no longer alone, and no longer afraid.

What is the difference between these two scenarios? Can you imagine how each situation ends? What happens to each of these residents? Why is one nursing assistant so different from the other? Which staff person would you want to care for you?

While the answers to these questions lie in a number of factors, the primary difference is an organization-wide philosophy of care. It is the creation of a culture that respects, prepares, educates and supports staff to work with the resident with compassion and love, as demonstrated in the second scenario. It is an environment committed to serving older adults, their families and the staff who work there. It is a facility where carefully selected and educated staff work together as a team, feel ownership, are heard, and have decision making opportunities and responsibilities. It is a respect-filled environment where staff is prepared, not just trained in the tasks of caregiving. They are knowledgeable about the aging process and are sensitive to the needs of older adults. In such an environment leadership is focused on service with a clear vision and mission where education, communication and inclusion are commonplace, and growth, innovation and compassion reside.

It is a facility that utilizes S.E.R.V.I.C.E.

INTRODUCTION _____

I have worked in the long-term care industry for almost two decades. Over the years, I found that there are facilities that are providing exceptional care and services to residents and their families - and others who are not. The excellent facilities tend to be pleasant places where residents and staff are happy and the environment is cheerful, clean and attractive.

But in sub par facilities, the residents are ignored, employees complain and grumble, and the environment is depressing. Staffing is a problem, and complaints from residents and families common.

Years ago, I began asking questions. What separates the good facilities from the bad ones? I have observed, explored and studied. In doing so I have learned that there are ways in which we can enhance these environments, the experience and the care that is provided. This book was motivated by a strong desire to help leaders change the experiences for residents, families and staff in long-term care facilities by implementing a leadership model that makes good places outstanding and turns sub par facilities into great ones.

If you are a leader in long-term care and your facility is full and making money, with good staffing levels and happy and satisfied residents, families and staff, you probably do not need to read any further. In addition, if you are happy and content in your work, finding yourself rising each morning excited about working another day in long-term care, you probably have already incorporated much of the information that will be discussed in this book.

However, many long-term care administrators are not consistently happy in their work. Faced with increasing competition, struggles with census, falling reimbursement, inadequate staffing, frequent complaints and disruptions, many of the designated leaders in long-term care feel ill-equipped to change their environments or deal with mounting issues. Unfortunately they often feel like mice on a wheel inside a cage, running as fast as they can and getting nowhere. If this describes you, this book will help you get off of the wheel and set a specific course and direction. Learning to lead will not only change your experience in the workplace but will also enhance the success of your facility.

Welcome, aboard. This book is for you.

Understandably, all organizations face a multitude of issues and problems. No one facility is alone or unique in such struggles. Yet, while some facilities are successful, others are failing. Why? Leadership, pure and simple. The premise of the book is this: a facility's success depends on the extent to which the principles and behaviors consistent with effective leadership are present in the daily operational life of the organization. Leadership can determine the success or failure of a facility or organization. Effective leadership, known to be a dominant force in successful businesses, is equally important in healthcare, and more specifically in long-term care. The application of effective leadership not only improves the bottom line for the organization, it also boosts the quality of life and work experience for all touched by long-term care.

The ideas and concepts contained in this book were derived from many sources. I have spent my entire career in health care, acute and long-term care and new project development. Over the past 18 years I have worked as a long-term care administrator which has enabled me to get an intimate perspective into the industry and its leaders. Direct involvement in the development and operation of the facility has provided a case study, furnishing a prototypical setting for the development, implementation and evaluation of a model of leadership. An extensive review of the leadership literature aided in the development of the model as well. A leadership survey for administrators was developed and completed in an effort to determine the current level of knowledge about popular leadership concepts and practices.

The ultimate purpose of this book is to encourage long-term care administrators to learn to lead. This book proposes a service-oriented leadership model that promotes more compassionate, effective and successful long-term care environments. The model presents an overarching organizational approach and philosophy of care under the direction of the responsible party and leader in long-term care - the administrator and CEO.

Each chapter includes a description of a theme and components, with examples of how they can be implemented in the day-to-day operations of a facility. Readers will be able to examine elements that comprise an effective model of leadership in long-term care, as well as find suggestions for programs and practices that will help in its implementation. Examples, in story format, provide both positive and negative practices and illuminate a practice or behavior that contributes to either wanted or unwanted outcomes. Examples are derived from actual experiences in various long-term care environments. This leadership model is simple and easy to understand, but its success depends upon a willingness to devote time to the development and implementation. Most importantly, a commitment to the work, staff, residents, family members and the facility itself is required to ensure success. Simply, the leader must be committed to S.E.R.V.I.C.E:

- **S**ervice-Care for others and put their needs first.

- **E**ducation-Educate and prepare people for their roles and promote ongoing education.

- **R**espect-Expect and demand respectful behavior of all.

- **V**ision-Know what is important to create.

- **I**nclusion-Ensure all voices are heard and each individual feels part of the larger collective.

- **C**ommunication-Take time to listen, provide and facilitate the exchange of information.

- **E**nrichment-Take care to know and nourish oneself.

Numerous authors have examined and discussed the importance and impact of leadership in business. While vast amounts of material are available about leadership in business, little is health-care based, and there is no literature available that discusses leadership in long-term care. This book is written with the goal of raising the awareness and importance of leadership in health care and long-term care.

Exploring Leadership

Effective leadership is key. It is particularly critical in times of change, uncertainty or fierce competition, all characteristic of the long-term care industry. Although an ineffective leader may have short-term success, maintaining success over a long period of time is extremely difficult, particularly in stressful, competitive climates. Arriving at a leadership position does not make one a leader. It is what the leader *does* in that position that makes the difference.

How a leader works affects employees as well. Employees in long-term care are different today and they know there are ample opportunities for employment. Staff members are neither frightened nor motivated by authority, and they are not driven by fear. Staff want to find a purpose and meaning in their work. They desire respect. They want to be heard and participate in the decision-making process. Employees want to grow and learn and are not satisfied with being told what to do without being told why.

It is a time of monumental change and challenges, when greater talents and strategies are needed to transform the long-term care industry. It is time for new and better leadership, one that moves beyond the 'business-as-usual mentality' or 'as it has been done in the past.' It is a new era, bringing increasing information, technology and challenges. How we operate our health-care institutions and facilities must change. Those who choose not to change may not survive. In this world of competitive health care, only the best will survive, and those with effective, visionary leaders will be the ones that dominate.

Long-term care is in a state of transition. Forces affecting long-term care, both in and out of the industry, are not in synch and in many cases work against one another. Meanwhile, the population grows increasingly older and lives longer. New and ever-changing rules and regulations, reimbursement strategies and cuts, policies and quality controls are thrust upon the industry, which is then forced to react. Why are industry leaders not a part of these decisions in the first place? Why are leaders forced to react to mandates that sometimes don't make sense or won't work? How can this dysfunctional, disconnected, inefficient system be changed? Most importantly, how can we improve care and the quality of life for the millions that this industry serves now and will serve in the future?

Leadership in Long-Term Care

Over the past two decades, the subject of leadership has received a great deal of attention in the business community, but it is inadequately addressed in the health-care literature. While bookstore shelves are lined with books on leadership, health-care literature that addresses leadership is rare. The limited material that does exist focuses on leadership in acute care, but is silent to leadership in long-term care. Even when leadership is mentioned in the long-term care literature, it is usually only the word 'leadership,' with little or no discussion about what it is, who it involves, or how to promote it.

In most of the long-term care literature, the administrator is not mentioned or identified when addressing new programs, interventions and even 'culture change.' It is as though the authors believe readers will 'just know' who is to be responsible for the programs and how to develop new organizations. Implementation is left up for grabs.

Similarly, when one examines textbooks utilized in the education of future long-term care administrators there are a few brief references to the importance of leadership and related theory. Authors may mention the word leadership, but do not define it, nor give guidance in establishing oneself as a leader. In addition, when discussing leadership, the components are more traditional, centering on discussion of power, lower and higher 'level' or 'echelon' employees. While deemed important, leadership is not addresses in relationship to developing oneself as a leader or implementing a leadership strategy.

Unfortunately authors do not comprehensively address how to provide leadership in an institution. Administrators are left to fend for themselves, coming into a job with the skill that they happen to bring and hope for the best. In essence, there is a critical component in long-term care that has yet to be explored, and that is leadership.

The Administrator as Leader

The Administrator is the leader in long-term care. Other people within the facility may take on a leadership role, but the administrator is ultimately responsible. It is the administrator whose license is on the line - and who ultimately determines the direction of a facility.

While change can be initiated in various places within the long- term care facility, the initiative will live or die in the hands of the person at the top, the administrator. Like it or not, a middle manager or a nurse alone will not change the organizational culture if it is not consistent with the desires of the administrator. It is the administrator's decision to allow new programs to be initiated and supported. It is the commitment of the administration to a program that determines its survival. As leaders of long-term care facilities, administrators have the ability to make these decisions and are in the best position to transform the industry.

The administrator is responsible for the daily operations of the long-term care facility. Administrators in this industry need to take a hard look at what they are doing and take responsibility for the environments that they create and for which they alone are responsible. It is up to them to choose their direction and determine their level of commitment. They must learn how to lead.

While it is important to look to the organizations that are responsible for the initial and ongoing education of administrators to improve upon the curriculum and provide more training in management and leadership, administrators need to realize that it is ultimately up to *them* to secure the necessary information and skills for leadership.

Management versus Leadership

Information about management and leadership has been a source of considerable interest over the past two decades, culminating in thousands of descriptions of management and leadership theories and systems. It is indeed a complex issue. Many believe managers and leaders serve two distinctly different roles. For some, management is about accomplishing a task, setting goals of an organization and focusing on the day-to-day concerns, while leadership is focused on the whole, the vision, the direction for the company and its people.

For the purpose of clarification, in this book managers and leaders are different. Managers are those who are mainly focused inside the organization, consumed with the day-to-day issues. They are occupied with procedures and how the staff is doing its work. The leader is focused on the whole; all operations, departments, strategies, internal and external climate, direction for the company, the vision and the plan for getting there. In long-term care, that would lie with the administrator. Managers in long-term care include all of the department directors, such as the director of nursing, director of dietary, director of environmental services, director of human resources and other management positions.

An Examination of Leadership

Many authors over the years have tried to identify the specific characteristics that make a leader successful. While an all-inclusive list would be overwhelming in length, some of the most frequently mentioned characteristics of leaders are that they are honest, trustworthy, focused, decisive, effective communicators, good listeners, open, creative, inspiring, competent and innovative. Although the list is long and some of the same characteristics are repeated by many authors, there is no universal list of leadership characteristics, despite numerous studies.

The debate continues about whether leaders are born or made. Some believe that an individual can be trained to be a leader. Others believe individuals are born with a specific talent that shows itself in a particular leadership position. Still others believe that some individuals are not born with this talent and all of the education and training in the world will not make that particular person a leader. Some authors believe that there are levels of leadership, that as a leader learns and develops they rise to more advanced levels of leadership. However, not all leaders will achieve the highest level because they are either unwilling to develop themselves further or not talented enough to do so. Thus, even leaders fall into various levels of achievement and expertise.

Evolution of Leadership

It is my belief that the definition and parameters of leadership have evolved. The more self-aware, contemplative and giving the leader becomes, the more advanced the leadership becomes. Leadership has moved away from a traditional, autocratic hierarchy, consumed by the financial success of the company and power of the leader. More recent leadership literature describes an environment that's sensitive to involving and including others within the organization through enhanced communication, empowerment, and opportunities to grow and learn.

There is an interesting parallel between the evolution of leadership and the evolution of humans theorized by Abraham Maslow. His theory describes a hierarchy, stages of development for humans. As the needs in each stage are met, the individual moves to a higher level of development. For many years, the highest level of achievement in Maslow's hierarchy was self-actualization. In his later years, Maslow believed that there was another level after self-actualization, composed of the individual's desire to serve others, to contribute to something bigger than himself.

What Maslow describes in human development is similar to what is seen in the development of leaders. Leaders are in various stages of development, which is why describing leaders and leadership is so difficult. We are not always talking about the same thing when we talk about leaders. A leader is not a position, but is a person with specific skills. I believe the more developed the person is as a human being, the more developed and effective he/she is as a leader.

One's ability to lead and their leadership knowledge will change over time as one learns in his/her work and life and grows. As in human development, a leader's basic needs, survival needs, must be met. Once these needs are achieved, an evolving leader moves on to the next stage of development, safety and security, enhancing his/her abilities as a leader. Some leaders get stuck in stages and never develop more fully, just as people do in life. Some people will enter a leadership position in a more advanced stage than others, thus their leadership abilities will be more seasoned. As Maslow described, humans operate at the level where their needs were met and, if threatened, would revert to an earlier stage until the need was once again met. I believe that the same happens in leadership, temporary moves may occur along the continuum. But continuous forward movement occurs only with additional work, experience and focused learning leading to a more evolved individual and leader.

Maslow describes the highest level of human development as one in which the human being seeks to be of service to others. This is also true in leadership. The highest level of human development and leadership development is the point at which an individual seeks to serve as a means of work and life. The individual at this stage of his/her development will be the most outstanding leader. Such individuals are the most developed internally - they know who they are, what is important to them in life, and are committed to serving others. They are passionate about their work and the people with whom they work. This is the highest level of leadership.

Thus the evolution described by Maslow applies not only to developing human beings, but also to the evolution of a leader (See Figure 1.). A leader may be in a position to satisfy basic needs, to obtain money for survival purposes, to be safe and secure. Once met, the leader moves to satisfy the need for recognition, often secured as power in leadership positions. Leaders then seek to belong and become more inclusive in their work. A leader who continues to work and grow will achieve self-actualization. The ultimate level is a service orientation in human development and leaders alike. When this is achieved, the human being/ leader is functioning at the highest level.

Figure 1.

Stages of Leadership Development Compared to Maslow's Hierarchy of Needs

STAGE	PROPOSED LEADERSHIP EVOLUTION	MASLOW'S HIERARCHY
6	Promotes and enforces a service-oriented environment-service to all, sees everyone as a customer	Transcendence, desire to do for others
5	Encourages growth and development of all and empowers staff	Self Actualization
4	Seeks input, listens to others and promotes teamwork	Belonging
3	More certain, self-assured leader, trusts self and others and is less afraid	Esteem
2	Begins to share information, no longer obsessed with power of position	Safety and Security
1	Leader by position, chance	Food and Water

A Working Definition of Leadership

Many authors have defined leadership in a variety of ways. In fact, there are hundreds of definitions of leadership.

In this book, leadership is defined as *the art of influencing and engaging colleagues to serve collaboratively toward a shared vision.*

Each part of this definition requires some explanation. First, leadership is an '*art*.' Not everyone is an artist, at least not automatically. Leadership, like art, requires education, exploration, experience and practice. This type of leadership is creative and innovative. It flows and takes special talent. Leadership talent requires a person who, like an artist, is willing to see things in a different perspective and encourages others to see it too. These leaders think outside of the box and envision something they eventually create.

'Engaging' is important, as leadership is more than a matter of influence. It involves getting people to care enough about the vision, job, and work to involve themselves, their hearts and souls in a vision. It is also about action, and the willingness for followers to put themselves into action for the vision. Initially the followers are intrigued, perhaps even enrolled, but in time, to be truly successful the followers must be engaged and committed. Once committed, they believe and share in the leader's vision, bringing with them their own contributions. Eventually the leaders and the followers become one with the vision, working together to strengthen and modify it over time, ensuring that the vision becomes truly operational. This shared grand plan serves as the foundation for all that is planned, developed and implemented in the organization.

The word *'colleagues'* places all of the members of the organization or team at the same level. Indeed, while there are individuals in various roles, all are important and necessary. They simply have different roles and responsibilities. In this model the organizational chart is flattened to recognize that all employees are equal and valued. While there has to be a system of authority for reporting or responsibility in decision-making and problem solving, that can be the system's sole purpose. A leader makes everyone feel as though they are at the top of the chart. While the use of "upper and lower levels" or "upper and lower echelon" has been used in the literature to describe individuals in various positions within an organization, this description runs counter to what this leadership model attempts to achieve. Consequently, the model proposes that all employees and customers of the organization are valued and important in accomplishing the goals and vision. There need not be a 'lower' and 'upper' or an 'us' and 'them,' just a 'we.'

'To serve' or serving others is ultimately the work of people in health care, and the reason that many individuals join the profession in the first place. The leadership model in this book is service-based: in the ultimate, everyday encounters with people whose needs must be met and who are to be served.

The word *'collaboratively'* describes the work and leadership model in action. It is more than cooperation. It is a team, with each individual contributing unique talents in such a way that all are used to accomplish the goals and vision. However, it is not just everyone doing their individual best work, it is about people coming together as one, doing whatever it takes to make it work, to create a culture or outcome consistent with the vision.

The most evolved leaders are visionaries who share the vision and keep the vision alive. They make the vision important, tangible, real and worthy of the effort. Leaders make the vision something the staff care about; something that they feel good about being a part of; something more important than just the individuals involved. The leader makes the vision one that is shared by all. The staff and the leader must share the vision, or the vision will never become a reality. If only the leader holds the vision for an organization, it will not be realized.

It is in the day-to-day tasks where the important work lies and the vision lives. The never-ending commitment to the vision, shown through actions everyday, is the key. Staff is engaged in the vision and continually improving the service or product, and the endeavor is truly collective. It is not about a vision statement printed on paper attached to the wall or typed on the back of a business card. It is about the staff as a collective team with a desire to serve, being part of the development of the vision and mission, and their commitment to living it everyday.

Why Define Leadership in Long-Term Care?

We have lost our way. Many in long-term care have forgotten what they were designed to do - to serve others by providing compassionate care for the older adults who can no longer be cared for in their homes. Over the years, the industry has changed, and not necessarily for the better. Recently we have begun to examine long-term care environments and ask for more than the current system provides. We are asking those who work in long-term care to evaluate their work and change the ways in which they comprehend and conduct their jobs.

We have also lost our focus. Multiple pressures and struggles have transformed the industry- growing numbers of sicker older adults needing health care services, excessive regulations, punitive surveys, increasing liability, growing competition, reimbursement cuts, lack of sufficient staff and questionable quality plague the industry. They have been allowed to consume all of our time, leaving little time for concentrating on the important task of serving. It is time to refocus and to reestablish service as our primary function.

For far too long society has complained, criticized, surveyed and regulated long-term care environments in the name of creating quality, to no avail. Care and compassion are not brought about by regulations or mandates, and are not found in the provision of a specific staffing ratio, reimbursement rate, or plush environment. Quality is found when service to others lives in the hearts of the people who work there. Ultimately, quality is created/ facilitated by the individual leader who is responsible for the operations of the facility.

Leadership that exists in many long-term care settings seems to happen by accident. In many cases there is no organizational perspective, and thus no overarching organizational plan. If there is a plan, few staff working there know about it. No one person is at the helm, nobody is driving the bus, many facilities lack direction and have no destination in mind. Many leaders simply come to work prepared to deal with the crisis of the day and that is all. It is important to examine the role of the leaders in long-term care, raise awareness of the impact of this position, encourage dialogue, and explore how to develop the role of leader in long-term care.

I recognize that the "leader" in long-term care is not always the Administrator. The focus here on the Administrator is to illuminate the position, as the administrator typically is the designated leader and certainly the one ultimately responsible by licensure for what happens in the facility. Thus the leader in long-term care is the Administrator. Although in some facilities, the administrator abdicates that role to others, including presidents, corporate personnel, Directors of Nursing, Assistant Administrators and other managers. Regardless of the whether the Administrator is leader or another serves as the leader, the development of an organization via this model the process is the same. This would also hold true for individuals who are designated leader for a specific project or unit within a facility, as long as they have the support of the administrator.

Hence the reality is that the designated leader, and in long-term care, is most often the licensed Administrator. In order to be successful, the Administrator must embrace this model and transformational process or get out of the way of others who choose to implement it. The hierarchical leader themselves may not be the one to create and implement all of the programs, but he/she must allow others in that leadership role to do so without interference.

Regardless of who ends up in the leadership position, the answer to success and high-quality human outcomes can be found not only in the operations of successful business and health-care organizations, but in the values, hearts and minds of administrators who are passionate about serving others and leading service-oriented facilities.

S.E.R.V.I.C.E.: A LEADERSHIP MODEL

This book and the model are aimed at helping administrators develop themselves and, ultimately, develop a culture of work and care fundamentally about serving others. In each of the key themes and comments, the ultimate desire is to serve others in some way. This service-oriented leadership model is comprised of seven components: service, education, respect, vision, inclusion, communication and enrichment/self-knowledge *(See Figure 2.)*

Overview of the Model

The foundation of this model of leadership is service. Many who write about leadership have talked about **service (S)** as a part of leadership motivation and experience. Serving others is the ultimate desire in this model.

Education (E) is proposed as additional training, internal or external, and most often to sharpen a worker's skills. But in this model, education takes on additional meaning as the basis of sustainable, ongoing programs of education and support and as a means of communication.

Respect (R) and garnering respect is what most health care workers regard as a most desired aspect of their work, but also identify as most lacking. In this model, respect is paramount.

Vision (V), a purpose, dream and destination for the organization, is believed by many to be essential to leadership. This vision creation is essentially about moving the entire organization in a strategic direction.

Inclusion (I) is discussed in different ways by many authors, and here includes mechanisms such as encouraging all to contribute, team building and empowerment. It is encouraging participation and ownership.

Communication (C) is important in getting people on board and keeping them there. It is a means of informing, tapping the knowledge, wisdom and experience of others and sharing it with all.

Enrichment (E) and self-knowledge have received attention as necessary components of effective leadership and here it is essential. Taking time to reflect and plan keeps a leader on a better course.

Figure 2.

S.E.R.V.I.C.E. Leadership Model

SERVICE
Using all gifts and talents to serve others and the vision.

- Working for a purpose higher than self with hope and optimism
- Serving others, rather than being served/seeing everyone as a customer
- Being a servant, teacher, coach, mentor, role model for others
- Living by the Golden Rule-Do onto others as you would have them do onto you
- Valuing the empowerment and growth of others
- Taking personal ownership of your work - "Running it like you own it"
- Caring about others

EDUCATION
Valuing and promoting education and learning as a lifelong process for self and others.

- Being skilled, knowledgeable, the best for self and others, the expert
- Providing educational mentoring and role modeling.
- Preparing staff for their roles
- Facilitating on-going personal and professional education and support programs
- Challenging and encouraging others to achieve goals and grow
- Choosing education over discipline
- Creating opportunities for collective learning

RESPECT
Valuing and promoting respect, dignity and personhood of others.

- Establishing respect as a core value
- Conducting all discussions in a private space
- Maintaining fair, consistent practices
- Treating all people with respect
- Recognizing and celebrating the accomplishments, contributions and successes
- Giving credit when and where due

VISION
Creating a total picture of what you dream of developing including guiding principles and values.

- Creating a vision, mission, and philosophy, being the best in the field
- Establishing guiding principles, values (trust, integrity, honesty)
- Looking at the whole vs. a part – systems thinking
- Planning-long term and short term vs. reacting to daily crisis
- Keeping the vision alive

S.E.R.V.I.C.E. Leadership Model

INCLUSION

Involving everyone as a partner in the evolution and progression of the project.

- Respecting, appreciating and recognizing the input and contribution of others
- Staying connected to staff
- Seeking the right persons and trusting them.
- Communicating expectations and requiring accountability
- Adopting a flat organizational chart philosophy
- Listening, supporting and teaching
- Promoting dialogue, formal and informal, honest and open

COMMUNICATION

Establishing an environment involving the active interchange of ideas and expectations.

- Communicating expectations and information to staff; increasing responsibility and accountability
- Remaining open and listening to comments, concerns and suggestions
- Creating opportunities to dialogue regarding new programs, innovations and solutions
- Surveying for initiatives to improve work experience and quality of care

ENRICHMENT

Generating self knowledge and conducting ongoing work with your self/spirit.

- Knowing who you are and what makes you tick – self-awareness
- Performing with integrity, maintaining personal values
- Listening to your inner voice, intuition
- Being open, having self-confidence and trusting in your own abilities
- Taking risks, trying innovative approaches, being confident, decisive, yet human
- Creating "balance" in your life
- Maintaining self through time for contemplation, reflection, introspection

The model is displayed in graphic form (See Figure 3.). This Service Leadership Model is based on an existing passion for the work and commitment to the organization. The hub of the model is service, which is at the heart of all of the other themes including education, respect, vision, inclusion, communication and enrichment.

All themes are interconnected and dependent upon one another. No single entity can stand as successfully by itself, but the introduction of any theme in practice will enhance an organization. Enrichment and self knowledge, for instance, includes ongoing education and is necessary for vision creation and maintenance, in turn enhancing the ability to serve others through the work. Being respectful is a means of serving others and drives a team mentality forging a more inclusive atmosphere. Communication is necessary in the establishment of the vision for the organization and all of the ongoing programs. The vision is necessarily service oriented, involving the provision of education, continued growth and learning promoting the inclusion of others in all efforts.

Service

The concept of service embodies working for the good or on behalf of others, often involving a purpose higher than oneself related to the vision and mission of the organization. When one sees all persons – residents, families and staff – as customers to be served and empowered, one changes the focus of the long-term care organization from survival to proactive optimism. Such a focus requires commitment to the remaining themes in the model, as the administrator role models personal ownership and responsibility to others. In this way, the administrator and management staff become teachers and coaches rather than those who hand out discipline. They are partners in the caregiving process, and remain mindful of the need to treat others in the manner that they wish to be treated.

Education

From the administrator to the housekeeper, individuals are often asked to come into a position with little education and no specific communicated expectations – yet they're expected to work successfully. When employees do not work up to standards, the fault is theirs, and they're considered lazy or not very bright. The fault, however, lies with the system, the facility, and the leader.

Administrators, as leaders, must educate and prepare employees appropriately to work in long-term care. Frequently individuals are hired and start their work without any orientation or training. It is imperative that staff be prepared for their new role, whatever it is. In many facilities, the only educational programs that are offered are those that are legislatively mandated. Staff members need to continue to learn, just as leaders do. Education programs must be diverse, routine, frequent and ongoing.

Respect

Long-term care staff is often not respected. They are not valued by the organization and are disrespectful to one another. In addition, they are not respected by a society that does not value aging and therefore dislikes all that comes with it, including long-term care. Society tends to demean those who work in long-term care as the "losers" in the healthcare industry.

Respect is lacking all around, from the administrator to the staff, staff to administrator and staff to staff. Families, residents, physicians and all others are also included in this mix. Respect is usually the first indicator staff mention when describing what they want and what they lack in their jobs. Leaders must acknowledge it, promote it and demand it to change the culture.

Vision

In an industry confused about its purpose, it seems that either nobody knows where they are going or are often going nowhere. There is no vision, mission, plan, or destination. People are simply coming to work, putting in hours, doing whatever they need to in order to get through the day and come again the next day to do the same.

Neither individuals nor the group is working toward a common vision or destination. Therefore, they are consumed by the crisis or concern of the day. While they might resolve a particular crisis that day, there is no picture of what they are trying to create long-term, no dream of what they want to become.

People need to know where an organization is headed. They want to know what they are working toward. It gives them purpose and pushes them to achieve. Leaders need to establish or enact a vision and mission for their facility.

Inclusion

In long-term care, the people who need to be involved in the decision-making process are seldom included. The folks doing the work are rarely asked for their input on new initiatives or programs, or how the work or work processes could be improved.

Staff members are not included in any of the decisions or plans for the organization. At best, they are informed only sporadically of the decisions that are made. In order to have a more efficient, well-run, successful facility, leaders need to include everyone involved in the organization in planning, problem solving and ongoing development.

Communication

Many things happen during the course of the day in a long-term care facility about which the staff needs to know. From information about a new admission to the planning for a dining room renovation, information when communicated can alleviate a great number of problems and enhance the activity.

Leaders need to establish a variety of mechanisms in which they and others can routinely communicate. This includes sending the information to staff and the equally important task of receiving information and feedback from the staff. Leaders must design and maintain efficient and effective communication systems.

Enrichment

As the leaders in long-term care, administrators are responsible for everything that happens in the facility and for the actions of all individuals in the facility. They work long hours and rarely leave the facility. Administrators have little quiet time and little time to think, reflect, or plan. Administrators must take time to care for themselves and encourage staff to do the same. They must continue to learn and grow, taking time for reflection and planning.

The Model

The following chapters describe each theme of the leadership model. Mechanisms for integrating each component into the long-term care system are discussed as a means of giving readers strategies for transforming their own environments. Individual themes may not seem new to individuals working in this field, but combined, provide a systemic organizational approach to changing the culture of long-term care. There is no one single program or practice that will transform every facility to a desired state. A combined approach must be embedded in the foundation of the operation.

SERVICE

Using all of your gifts and talents to serve other and the vision.

- Working for a purpose higher than self with hope and optimism.

- Serving others, rather than being served; seeing everyone as a customer.

- Being a servant, teacher, coach, mentor, and role model for others.

- Living by the Golden Rule.

- Valuing and empowering the growth of others.

- Taking personal ownership in your work. Running it like you own it.

- Caring about others.

Joan

Joan was the day shift cook in the kitchen, normally arriving at 6 A.M. and leaving her shift at 2:30 P.M.   One evening Joan was working late and when asked what she was doing at work so late, said that she was helping a resident. One of the residents with dementia refused to eat.   Multiple strategies had been used to get this resident to eat; changing environments, securing and sending all her favorite foods, feeding her at numerous times of the day and evening.   Even the family came in to support her and brought foods they had prepared for her.   Still she would not eat.

One day Joan made a special delivery to the resident's room and talked with her.   The resident lit up and seemed to recognize and care for Joan, although they had never met. Suddenly she started eating.   However, she would only eat if Joan encouraged her.   No other staff or family member could do what Joan could do. Joan was coming in daily in the evenings to see that the resident ate dinner.   Though working at the facility during the day, she came in evenings on her own time and on days off to encourage the resident to eat. She never told anyone, and never asked for anything for herself - another quiet hero in long-term care.

Anna

Late one night, Anna, an evening shift aide, was seen in the facility after midnight, looking stressed and weary. When asked why she was still there and what was wrong, she said she was taking turns with another nursing assistant, sitting with Mrs. Smith who was dying. Mrs. Smith's family could not be with her and they did not want her to die alone. The two nursing assistants had decided to take turns on their own during their time off. Although they had to work the next day, they insisted on staying. Mrs. Smith died at six in the morning...with Anna by her side.

In health care and long-term care, it is assumed that the primary job is to care for others, or in other words, to serve others. Yet a service-oriented culture is not what many people experience in health-care environments today. They do not consistently experience a service-oriented culture or a caring and compassionate staff. While there is a great deal of discussion about service, there seems to be a lack of understanding about how to create such a culture organizationally.

Service involves providing and caring for others. Service has several facets; it can be the desire to serve, the fulfillment of an obligation, and for some, a duty or a 'calling.' In leadership, the desire to serve is recognized as an important component for success. Service-oriented leadership involves putting the needs of others before one's own, finding ways to meet those needs, and recognizing other individuals' worth and value. It is offering oneself to others.

Service in this model is when leaders use all talents to serve and to fulfill an obligation to others and the vision and mission of the organization. The driving force for these leaders is working for something more important than themselves, something that will make a difference in the lives of others. The leader in this service model wears many hats, including colleague, guide, helper, teacher, coach, mentor, facilitator, role model and cheerleader.

Service is at the hub of this leadership model. The desire to serve is at the heart of the other components addressed in this model. In this model, leadership *is* service.

Working for a Purpose

It is important to identify the purpose of the work in long-term care. Certainly, it is to care for older adults with physical and cognitive needs that can no longer be met in their homes. The purpose is not only to care for the physical aspects, but also to promote enhanced mental and spiritual well-being.

Another purpose is to ease the burden for families. Being available when others need help and providing services is geared toward the needs of families. Staff needs to be available any time of the day or night to assist families of current and potential future residents. Needs of families providing care at home can occur at any time – they don't conveniently happen between the hours of 9:00 AM and 5:00 PM. Education and support programs for families help them cope with the frailness and changes in someone they love.

An equally important purpose of service is to create a respectful, supportive, and meaningful environment for staff. Staff is key to the success of a facility. They need to be respected, educated, supported and included in the organization. That will entail staff members understanding their purpose, the importance of their work, and the difference that they can make.

Serving Others as Customers

Administrators need to recognize that everyone who comes into contact with their facility is a customer who forms an impression of them and their work by the encounter. Most likely, they will tell others whether that encounter was good or bad. A sales person, a deliveryman, a neighbor, a student, a potential employee and anyone else should be viewed as someone you are there to assist. Your reputation, your ability to have a good census and recruit and retain staff depends upon how well each person is treated by you and your staff.

Make certain that everyone's needs are addressed, by you or by a member of your staff. Educate the staff on this issue and let them know it is an expectation. From kindness, attentiveness, and assistance on the phone to assisting a stranger in the lobby, all staff should ask how they may help them.

Serving the residents starts with providing a respectful and dignified atmosphere. The residents are adults, having led full lives with numerous accomplishments. Each resident is somebody's loved one, a mother, father, brother or sister. They are judges, lawyers, businessmen and women, wives, mothers, world travelers, teachers, cooks, somebody special to someone. The residents deserve all the respect that any other person should expect. It also includes an individualized approach to care, ensuring that the person is the focus of the staff's work.

Families struggle to cope with their situations. Some families seem to accept what is happening to their family member while others never will. Some feel sad, others angry, others guilty. Without knowing the history and the dynamics of each family, it is important to make this experience the least traumatic that it can be. In serving residents and families, all decisions should be made to benefit residents and families, rather than the convenience of the staff and facility. Every decision needs to be evaluated from the perspective of an individual resident or family member.

Staff members are also customers. You need to serve them if you expect to secure and keep quality personnel. If you want staff to provide good care, take good care of them. Establish programs to prepare them, support growth and development, the sense of satisfaction and accomplishment, and the discovery of personal benefits from serving others in their work and lives.

Serving the community includes being a source of information, referral and support. Encourage people to call even if they only have a question and even if they will not utilize services. It is valuable to the organization to help everyone who requests assistance.

Being a Servant, Teacher, Mentor, Coach and Role Model

In this model, a leader is to first be of service. Leaders look at what can be done for others and see that their needs are met. The role of such a leader in long-term care is to determine how to serve the customers: residents, families, staff and others in contact with the facility. The leader's involvement in that process is to be a part of the service team and, in effect, be one who is doing the serving. If a leader is not involved in the provision of the service, how can he/she know what needs people have and how to meet them? Working with staff enhances the leader's knowledge, not only of the needs of the residents and families, but also of the staff. Long-term care provides a service. If it is to be a consistently good service, a leader must be in the midst of it, evaluating and determining that the service provided is what was envisioned.

Consequently, leaders will find themselves serving as teacher, mentor and coach. It is up to leaders to educate staff about what is needed, what is envisioned and how to get there. Part of the job of a long-term care leader is to teach - to educate managers and to be involved in the education of the direct-care staff. Managers must be educated not only in the skills required for the position, but the values, vision and direction of the organization. Managers in turn, assist in teaching others and offering a consistent message.

As a mentor, especially to managers, a leader teaches and counsels on how to perform work and deal with issues on the job. Many managers in long-term care are placed in positions with no training and are expected to perform. They are unfamiliar with how to teach, communicate and problem-solve. The leader's role becomes one that facilitates growth.

The leader is the most important role model, for what the leader does affects everyone in the organization and every person the organization touches. In this role, the leader sets the stage and determines how people will act and how much they care. The entire staff looks to the leader to lead and to show them how to act. Employees watch the leader constantly, to evaluate how he/she handles a situation, and to see if actions are consistent with his/her words. Leaders must be conscious and consistent with all that they do and say.

Living by the Golden Rule

Good service and customer-oriented service are best understood through one's own eyes. The best way to get staff members to understand the impact of service is to ask them to look at each situation from their own perspective, as if it were happening to them. A guide for their decisions and actions is to ask how they would want to be treated. What kind of environment would they like to live in? What kind of food would they like to eat? When would they like to get up and how late would they stay up? How would they like to be treated and handled by another? It is important to repeatedly discuss situations, activities and events from this perspective, asking how staff would like it to be if it were for their own family members.

This process also includes how to treat families, students, visitors, volunteers and each other. From answering the phone to greeting a visitor, it is important to examine the process and ask staff to think about how they would feel and what would make them most comfortable. Once their level of awareness is raised, how staff wants to be treated dictates how they treat others.

Valuing Empowerment and Growth of Others

When leaders are service-oriented, they are committed to those they lead and value them as individuals. Once leaders have given others the knowledge and tools to do their job and set expectations, allowing them to do that job and to make decisions is the leaders' way of trusting and empowering them. This should include all staff at all levels of the organization.

Prepare staff for their job, emphasizing standards and expectations and then allow each person to do their job. The decisions an empowered staff member will make may not always be the same as the one the leader would make, but this is a learning and growth process. If a staff member makes a poor choice, it is an opportunity to teach, to talk with them about alternative decisions that could have been made and why. Teach and guide them to make a better decision in the future. Staff needs to be given the freedom to take action and make the necessary decisions for the residents. Do not belittle or scold staff for a poor decision. If you do, they will not make decisions on their own again, and the organization will not grow. One person cannot be expected to make all decisions all of the time. Progress is a collective endeavor.

In addition, it is very rewarding for a leader to see the growth of others. Most of the time when leaders trust in others and give staff a chance, they will exceed expectations. True leaders need to care about their staff and help them achieve their highest potential. In turn, staff cares about the leader and the organization and wants to do the best they can.

Take Personal Ownership

An effective leader is passionate and believes in something so strongly, they invest all of themselves in the success of the organization and vision. In essence, they work as if they own it. Invested first in the vision, these leaders go about creating it without thought of the time, energy and personal sacrifices. It is bigger and more important than what they plan to get out of it.

When the leader takes on the responsibility as owner, the staff see and experience that. They in turn will invest more of themselves in the process, too. They put forth the same enthusiasm and dedication as if the facility belonged to them. They do take it personally.

Caring About Others

Effective leaders care about others. They do not become best friends and shouldn't, but leaders take the time to know and care about others. Not only do those around benefit when you take the time and energy to care for others - you will, too. The more you care and give, the more that comes back to you. A caring attitude on the part of the leader increases the likelihood that others on staff will care as well.

Successful leaders take the time to know the residents, their families and the staff. They even schedule time to be in the facility to encourage relationships. Leadership is the cultivation of relationships.

 FREQUENTLY ASKED QUESTIONS

This seems so hard and time consuming. How will I ever find the time?

You *decide* to make the time. It is a choice. Effective leaders do so because it is important to them to develop a service-oriented environment. Remember, you are building something. It is like building a house. It takes a lot of time, planning, energy and activity at the start. When the house is complete, you can relax and enjoy it. You may decorate and make improvements from time to time, but the foundation is in place. It is the same with service and the model. Once the model is in place and the staff is functioning with the vision in mind, your time commitment will diminish tremendously.

How do I go about defining service?

First, you need to spend some quiet time as the leader, defining service for yourself.   What is it?   How does it look in your organization and how does it feel?   What is service to residents? How can you best serve families, staff and the community?   Once you have defined it for yourself, you should meet with one or more of the management team.   Select individuals with whom you have the greatest level of comfort.   Ask them to define service as well, share your ideas and brainstorm.   Meet with the rest of the management team and do the same.

When you feel comfortable with your decisions, then meet and share ideas with the rest of the staff.   Ask them to define service and listen to what they say.   Encourage them to add to your definitions and list of ideas. Do so until you can come to agreement on a consistent definition of service for your organization.

How do I determine whom we serve?

Take this definition of service and make a list of whom you serve and how you serve them.   Discuss it with managers and staff and expand as appropriate.   In long-term care it is going to include residents and families. This model suggests that management and leadership are in place to help educate and serve the staff. If you intend for your staff to provide good care to residents and families, you need to take good care of them as well.   If you don't, in time they will not stay.

 Staff is also there to take care of each other.   This will be a new concept for many who have not seen this as part of their responsibility or an expectation.   Make it one; they have much to contribute to the success of the team and the success of future employees.

If you are a facility that is a clinical setting for students, you are there to serve them.   Make it a *positive* experience for students.   Establish preceptors who will look over them and see that they are treated well.   If you do they will tell others, especially other health care professionals. Such a positive environment encourages students to apply for long-term care positions in the future and is an effective marketing device.

Once established and identified, discuss service routinely in staff meetings throughout the year. Remind staff of what they decided was important in the service to others. In the midst of all of the activities in a long-term care facility service can get lost. You have to consistently keep service foremost in their minds in an effort to see it in their work.

What if I encounter or receive a complaint about bad service after I have educated the staff?

Of course you will get complaints, but the greater the education and communication, the fewer complaints you will receive because staff will know what to do, how to do it, and what the expectations are of the organization. First, listen to families and complaints, and ensure them that you will look into it and take appropriate action. Then check out the complaint with staff. Depending on the outcome, perhaps the staff needs more information, education, or supplies. Remain non-judgmental until you know all of the information. Then, think education before discipline.

When you encounter poor service as a customer or consumer in another facility or business use it as an example as you train and educate your staff. Talk with employees about the event and encourage them to talk about how they would conduct themselves in a different manner.

What if I have a staff person who refuses to care or change?

Once you have given them all the education and support that you can, you have little choice but to ask them to leave. Negative, consistently argumentative staff will pull down the morale of the entire staff and create much more work for you and management. Poor attitudes are counterproductive and will slow the process. Your unwillingness to tolerate such behavior is often appreciated by the rest of the staff and demonstrates your commitment to this way of working together.

The desire to be of service to others will be played out in many ways. After deciding first to serve others, another important component of the model is to serve others through the provision of education. The next chapter will describe the education program and the importance of education to the organization.

EDUCATION

Valuing and promoting education and learning as a lifelong process for self and others.

- Being skilled, knowledgeable, the best for self and others the expert.

- Providing educational mentoring and role modeling.

- Preparing staff for their roles.

- Facilitating on-going personal and professional education and support programs.

- Challenging and encouraging others to achieve goals and grow.

- Choosing education over discipline.

- Creating opportunities for collective learning.

Only a Building

It was a multi-million dollar building, with a brand-new dementia unit. The development team had studied designs, attended workshops and traveled throughout the county looking at dementia units so that they would build the very best. It was a popular design, contained the best furniture and a combination of all of the elements that other units had identified as beneficial, including resident "memory boxes" and an aviary. Coming soon was an entire spectrum of plants and animals. Why wasn't it working? Why was the staff unwilling to stay, and why was the turnover so high? Why was it chaotic and noisy all of the time? When a consultant asked about the education and support programs, the answer was this: there wasn't enough time or money.

No Education

An administrator had opened an Alzheimer's disease unit about a year and a half ago and was still having tremendous problems with staff burnout and turnover. He paid the staff on the unit more than anywhere else in his facility and could not understand what the problem was. Now he was being cited for multiple resident care issues, many of which had occurred on the unit. When questioned about the education of the staff he said, "Oh, they are educated. They all went through that class; they are all certified."

The purpose of education is to give staff the necessary information and skills to be successful. It is an opportunity as well to communicate organizational expectations. It also lets staff know that they are valued. Yet, even though many healthcare administrators believe in the idea, many view education as commanding too much time or too great an expense. Long-term care administrators cannot afford to avoid or delay providing education when it is critical to the transformation of an environment. The results of educational programs often include organizational change, improvements and enhanced care.

Effective leaders are committed to ongoing personal and professional education and support programs for themselves and those they lead. Leaders value education and learning as a lifelong process. It is required when preparing to be the best, to deliver the best care, to become the expert. It involves challenging others to grow and achieve. This educational philosophy is a process that encourages teaching as an opportunity to build and strengthen the team and organization through creating moments of collective learning.

Being Skilled and Knowledgeable

Supporting education starts with the leader valuing self-education and self-knowledge. Leaders need to exhibit skills and knowledge in the field in which they work and stay on the cutting edge of what is happening in the field. This does not mean that leaders must know everything. Leaders who can't answer a question only need to be willing to look for the answers.

In health care and especially long-term care, understanding the clinical experience as well as the textbook knowledge is important to merging academia and practice. Leaders in long-term care must be knowledgeable in both. If they are not practical in their approach to applying the information they learn, they will lose the followers. If what they know intellectually cannot be put into practice, what difference can the information make? People will follow leaders only if they believe in their knowledge and their abilities, and only if those leaders put what they have learned into practice.

Frequently, positive results from research-based interventions in long-term care cannot be maintained over time in practice. The intervention probably was not practical, operationally feasible, nor affordable in the first place. A researcher who initiates a project may have the knowledge about how to improve care, but possess little or no awareness about the daily operations of a facility. As a result, the intervention will succeed but fail to be sustainable.

For instance, an Associate Professor from a local university wanted to enhance the knowledge of the nursing assistants regarding sensory losses in aging. She came to the facility with a plan and curriculum. The curriculum was wonderful, yet the plan became a failure. She wanted to provide six two-hour sessions, given in one session per week on Wednesdays from 12:00 to 2:00 P.M. There were several issues identified by staff as problematic. First, why did the program address only nursing? Why not include all staff, since all staff come into contact with the residents? The timing was also an issue. It was planned to conduct sessions during the lunch hour. But, how were staff to attend if they were assisting residents with lunch? In addition, what provisions would be made for staff on other shifts? Finally, two hours was not only seen as too long to be away from the residents, even if staff did so in shifts, but it was longer than the staff said that they were willing to sit and listen.

The instructor learned a great deal from this, especially when the staff worked out an alternative means of getting the information. They decided on less material, presented in half-hour sessions that would be delivered to staff on all three shifts by the professor and a department manager. The programs were conducted and enjoyed by all participants. It is up to the facility to implement an educational program that is ongoing and sustainable.

Education serves to be more than just training and skill development. It is a means of encouraging growth and development of staff in their work and in life. A commitment to education and to continued learning as individuals and as an organization indicates the organization's commitment to enhanced performance.

Educational Mentoring and Role Modeling

Leaders and management educate staff by serving as role models. Actions truly speak louder than words and, rest assured, the staff is watching. How you handle stress and difficult situations becomes a model for the staff. If an administrator yells at someone in public, employees will do the same. If managers are short and curt, staff will be, as well. If leaders do not show that they care for the residents or families, or are disrespectful in any way, they should not expect staff to show any compassion or respect either. The leader sets the tone. If leaders are absent and do not care, staff won't care either. Leaders are responsible for an uncaring and uninvolved staff.

The same holds true with the management staff and supervisors. It has been established that the number one reason a person leaves a job is dissatisfaction with a supervisor. It is up to the leader not only to be a role model but also to set the tone and behavior of managers and/or supervisors. Most do not come with training in this area. Leaders must seek ongoing training and take the time to teach the management and supervisory staff. It may take many one-on-one meetings and educational programs on how to manage and supervise others. It is time well invested. Managers will learn how to manage the staff in a more respectful and effective way.

Managerial education also requires working with managers and supervisors to examine situations from a different perspective. When things go wrong, managers should be asked to look at it as an opportunity for teaching, not discipline. Most of the time staff want to do things right. They just don't know how. Staff does things in a particular way because they have 'always done it that way.' They are unaware of other options. Sometimes staff is unclear about what is expected of them. When a mistake is made, it is a time to determine if expectations have been clearly communicated or if the staff has had enough direction, orientation or education.

Education is important to the growth and success of the staff and the organization as a whole. The more an organization learns, the more capable they are of providing the best service to others. By necessity, this includes identifying not only individual mistakes but also systemic problems and learning to develop solutions collectively. When an organization takes an educational approach to problems and their solution, leaders and staff have an invaluable opportunity to learn from past encounters and history. Otherwise, they will be destined to repeat the same mistakes over and over again.

Preparing Staff for Their Roles

Lack of an orientation program creates problems for staff and residents. Inadequate orientation is often a frustration for staff and a reason that they leave a job. It leaves a staff feeling ineffective, insufficient and discouraged, frequently leading to turnover. All too often, employees are expected to function perfectly without any information about what to do or what is expected. Initial orientation and training is essential for preparing a new employee for their work. It is an opportunity to instill the vision, values, standards and expectations. How does a new employee function when no one has described expectations for work and behavior?

An initial orientation should last for at least two weeks and include time spent on the unit working with a mentor as a team with residents. The amount of prior experience does not alter the time or information that each new employee requires during orientation in a new facility. Orientation should not be optional. Every department manager should be responsible for seeing that the orientation is complete. In some cases an employee may need more than two weeks. Supply what is necessary to see that staff receives what they need individually. To do otherwise is to doom the employee to failure.

Facilitating On-Going Education and Support

Family Education

Educating families early in the admission process will also alleviate work down the road. They need to understand long-term care, what they can expect and where to go with questions, concerns, and problems. Informing families of the routine, the best time to visit or call will enhance their ability to get the information they need without being disruptive to the staff and facility operations.

Families often come with little information about what is happening to their loved one, especially families dealing with dementia. Educating families individually or in groups serves to enhance their understanding of the disease, their family member's behavior, and what may come in the future.

Ongoing education for families is important to help families understand what is happening and what to expect. A structured educational venue, such as routine family meetings, decreases the frequency of individual questions and concerns, and resulting disruption of daily operations. This also serves as a mechanism for keeping in touch with family thoughts, observations and concerns.

Staff Education

Ongoing education and support programs are essential in ensuring staff effectiveness. The educational needs do not end with the completion of orientation. Issues, questions and problems will surface in time and new information will become available to share with staff. Weekly education and support meetings serve to meet the educational and support needs of staff. These meetings should take place on the various shifts and repeated two or more times each shift to enable all staff to attend and for the ease and convenience of staff.

This specific education and support program involves developing and conducting in-service programs every week on all three shifts. Department managers and administration take turns assuming responsibility for the educational content and implementation, dependent upon their area of expertise. The management team, along with the staff, should develop a list of potential topics. Once selected, the programs should be posted each month for the upcoming month. The programs can be conducted on one particular day during the week to bring some consistency to the event. Staff can count on that day and plan accordingly. Programs should last no more than half an hour. The same individual should lead the program on all three shifts to ensure continuity.

Many subjects should be addressed annually, including vision/mission, specific job skills, time management, normal aging, sensory changes in aging, Alzheimer's disease and dementia, how to handle specific behaviors, communication strategies, working with families, team building, managing conflicts, etc. One week each month, for example, might be devoted to stress management or mechanisms for working better together as a team. On occasion in-services could include entertaining and fun events such as car maintenance, cake decorating or flower arranging.

The sessions should be planned and posted in advance, but subject to change quickly. In response to facility needs, there are occasions when the educational content is determined by the needs of the staff at the time. For instance, if a resident is admitted with a specific disease not usually dealt with in the facility, an educational program should be designed to educate the staff about that disease. Or if the staff is having some problems working together, it may be time to do an educational program on mechanisms for working collaboratively.

Programs are not only of educational value, but provide an excellent opportunity to stay connected to staff and to solicit ideas. Staff will relay concerns and issues at this time, as well. The person responsible for conducting the educational program should provide feedback to the management team or any individual department manager as needed. Staff may have shared information about issues with a particular resident's behavior, concern about a family member, or lack of supplies. While voiced in the meeting, the information can be shared with the specific department manager or the entire management team as appropriate. Whatever the issue, there are ample opportunities to discover concerns when routine meetings are held.

Nurses, managers and administration should attend the educational in-services. They too will learn from the material presented and it serves as an opportunity for them to hear what staff, from all departments, has to contribute. It demonstrates that they value learning and serves to model commitment to the concept. Attendance is a valuable opportunity to connect and spend time with staff, promoting camaraderie.

Managers and staff members become very creative in their approach to education and training. For instance, a director of nursing who conducted a program on infectious disease used a Jeopardy game approach, with questions, answers and gifts for the winners. A director of activity programming educated the staff about the importance of activities and outings for the residents when he took staff in small groups on a bus ride and for ice cream as though they were going with residents. To add variety to the weekly events, one manager trained staff on how to surf the Internet. Another manager, trying to get the staff to understand the impact of the physical environment for families and visitors, took pictures of different sights in the facility that they wanted staff to notice, to help them see the environment through the eyes of the family or a visitor. Staff members were able to experience the impact of trash on the floor, and a cluttered hallway with hampers and empty wheelchairs. It made a major impact on the staff and was used to remind everyone of the importance of the physical environment.

In addition to department managers and administration, there are others in the community willing to add to the educational programs provided in a facility. Local universities and colleges are excellent sources of information and speakers. Students are often willing to research a topic and conduct an educational program that in many cases is a requirement for the student's education. Physicians, researchers, senior adult organizations, therapists and vendors provide programs on topics of interest to staff. All they need is an invitation.

Everyone is a teacher and a student. While a single individual conducts the educational programs, everyone participating has the capacity to teach and to learn. This philosophy encompasses the belief that everyone is valued and what he or she has to contribute is valuable, as well. The expectation is that everyone will contribute, teach, learn and grow.

Informal Opportunities for Education

Both formal and informal educational events are valuable. Formal programs are those that are planned and scheduled with a specific agenda. Equally important are the informal opportunities for education for managers and administrators that arise simply by walking through the facility. If someone is doing something wrong or that could be done differently, this is an excellent opportunity to teach. For instance, if a nursing assistant is having difficulty getting a resident with cognitive impairment to perform a task, this presents a chance to work on alternative strategies with the staff person. It is an opportunity to give them an array of possibilities so that the next time a similar situation occurs they will have more than one strategy for working with such a resident. They will not forget this information, but will use it for future encounters.

An effective educational strategy is for management and administration to be physically close to the resident care areas. In fact, it is my belief that the best facility design would be for all management and administrative offices to be interspersed within the resident care areas. It forces management and administration to see and be aware of what is going on daily, versus being isolated in offices making judgments about situations of which they are not aware or have not experienced. Spending time in the resident care areas also facilitates a sense of teamwork. When administrators and managers are involved, they can't help but stop and be of assistance. They get to know the residents, families, and staff much better.

Although this program is time-consuming, it is worth the effort. Some may say that they cannot afford the time to follow such a plan. I believe that they cannot afford not to provide these programs. Educational programs will prepare and make the staff more successful in their work. This will benefit the residents, the staff, families and the facility. In addition education and learning is interesting and motivating. The staff members enjoy learning and as a result of this new information, they will generate better solutions to problems. This educational effort also indicates to the staff that management cares, and that they are willing to invest time and energy in the staff.

Challenging and Encouraging Others to Achieve and Grow

Leaders must encourage education in the facility and programs outside of the facility. It does the staff a world of good to attend programs in other locations. They meet other individuals in their field and have the opportunity to examine how others deal with their work. They, too, will learn from others and enjoy the process. Meetings held in other facilities, state associations, national meetings and business oriented meetings offered by organizations such as local chambers are wonderful opportunities for exposure. Staff will come back to the facility and share what they have learned with others. Their spirits are lifted; they are stimulated and refreshed.

One administrator who operates a facility in the Georgia sends some of his staff every year to a national meeting. Direct care providers and management attend this meeting together, so management is available to guide and entertain the staff. They fly them to the meeting and pay all expenses. For some of the staff, it is the first time they have been on a plane. Reportedly, everyone who goes enjoys this trip. It supports their desire to learn and speaks highly of how much staff is valued.

Encourage involvement in the community for the benefit of the staff as well. Support their involvement with their professional organizations, boards, or volunteer groups within the community. Doing so facilitates the learning and growth of the individual who in turn becomes a teacher for other staff in the facility. Involvement facilitates new learning, the ability to share information with others. It also serves to enhance the visibility and awareness of the facility to individuals and organizations in the community.

Choosing Education Over Discipline

To help people be successful in their work, first they must be educated. They need to understand what their jobs entail, how they are to be conducted and what the expectations are. So often it is assumed that people in long-term care already know all of this without being told. They are expected to come on the job and begin. When they don't do things exactly the way expected they are disobedient, lazy, or negligent.

When examining this phenomenon, it is important to determine not only what a person may have done improperly, but why. Did they know what to do? Were they familiar with how to do it? Were they aware of the facility's standards of care and practice?

Not only do leaders need to educate all employees as they enter a new job; the education process is one that should never end. The point is, leaders will only get out of someone what they put into them. Leaders must be willing to put some time and energy into those with whom they work.

Creating Opportunities for Collective Learning

Just as with visioning as a group, learning as a group elevates the outcome. It is enhanced by the input of others. Much more can be learned in a group, when people are respected and valued for their contributions.

All of the educational programs, formal and informal, are opportunities for collective learning. Being open and listening to the voice of others from all departments and all positions is a wonderful chance to see an issue, problem or plan from a variety of perspectives in a much more complete way.

Opportunities for collective learning create opportunities for collective communication and feedback. A commitment to routine learning sessions enhances communication and gives a good basis for knowing the tone, mood and needs of all of the staff in the facility. It provides information in heading off potential problems.

In addition, group-learning experiences are fun and facilitate relationships, the basis of creating successful teams and quality work. When people get to know one another as individuals, they can work better together, and are more supportive of one another.

FREQUENTLY ASKED QUESTIONS

What can I do to become more skilled and knowledgeable as a leader?

It is an ongoing, never-ending process. You need to take the time to educate yourself. Read books in and outside the industry. Attend educational programs of interest or those in which you will develop a skill. When attending educational program, conventions, trade shows, attend the sessions looking for best practices. Get out of the facility! Network and attend programs in other industries and businesses. Join the local Chamber of Commerce, as many businesses have similar issues. Such events provide opportunities to learn from others in and out of the industry.

I need staff on the floor now. How can I send them to orientation?

You can't afford NOT to spend time with staff in orientation. It is a time to set up expectations, discuss practices, standards and values of the organization. It eases their transition into the facility as they are introduced to people and processes. They will know where to go for information and help. How comfortable would you be if thrown into a job? And if you have been, was it a positive or stressful experience? The more comfortable they are, the better their performance and longevity.

The education programs are very time consuming. How do I find the time?

While education programs may seem time-consuming, they represent time well spent and serve multiple purposes. Educational programs are designed to increase knowledge or skills, but also serve to be an opportunity to spend time with staff. It enhances your ability to determine staff morale. It also says that you value staff, taking time to go out of your way to do more for them.

Educational programs, half-hour in length and presented multiple times over a day, can be presented by a variety of people. Department heads and administration alone allows for a number of programs. There are also students, vendors and other health care professionals willing to conduct programs; they just need to be asked.

What is a staff support program?

It is an educational opportunity to teach staff how to care for themselves and deal with the stress in their work. It will also enhance their ability to deal with the daily issues confronted in their own personal lives. It might include a presentation on the effects of stress and the benefits of exercise. Other topics for consideration include guided imagery, meditation, tai chi, yoga and other stress reducing strategies.

Once educated individuals are better equipped to work, cope with stresses, and be more successful. With increased knowledge they are also in a better position to contribute to groups and to the organization promoting ideas for improvement and ways in which they accomplish their work. It behooves leaders to take advantage of this information and talent.

RESPECT

Valuing and promoting respect, dignity and personhood of others.

- Establishing respect as a core value of the facility.

- Conducting all discussions of behavior and corrective action in a private space.

- Maintaining fair, consistent staff relations practices, treating all staff with respect, regardless of position.

- Recognizing and celebrating staff accomplishments, contributions and successes, giving credit where credit is due.

An Ill-Informed Expert

In a recent article about "the staffing crisis" another 'expert' compares the nursing assistant's job choice and level of compensation to working at a fast food restaurant. It is so degrading. It is as though the nursing assistant's decision was based on a desire for turning hamburgers, rather than turning human beings. One would wonder if the writer had spent much time talking to individuals working in long-term care. Many nursing assistants don't make decisions about where they will work based on money alone. They don't all decide to go into long-term care because they can make an extra 25 cents an hour. Staff members are involved in this work because they care. They get satisfaction from making a person's life a little happier and more comfortable. They are proud of their accomplishments and pleased to make a difference in the life of another human being. They deserve more respect than they often receive.

Sarah

A nursing assistant was late again. The Director of Nursing was angry. After all, she had verbally counseled this employee on several occasions.

She had changed Sarah's shifts to accommodate the employee's scheduling problems. In fact, she had even given Sarah a grace period in which to report to work to decrease the occurrence of tardiness. On this occasion, the nursing assistant walked in and the Director of Nursing immediately started yelling at her in the lobby of the facility. This occurred in front of her nursing colleagues and individuals from other departments. The nursing assistant tried to explain that a policeman had stopped her for speeding on the way to work. She had been speeding so that she would not be late. The Director would not listen. She simply walked away. Crying and upset, Sarah quit and walked out, on the spot. She was too embarrassed to stay. The Director had to stay that evening and work the assignment of the nursing assistant until a replacement could be found. The remaining staff was sad. They had lost a quality assistant, colleague and friend.

Respect is often an indicator used in defining a good working environment. It entails valuing the feelings, dignity, needs and uniqueness of another. This involves not only taking these into account in how we treat others on a regular basis, but also acknowledging individual contributions to fulfilling the mission of the organization. The desire for respect is universal. Although respect would seem to be a basic, logical ingredient to the treatment of others, it is unfortunate that respect in the workplace is a topic that continues to require attention. Clearly, as reported by many health care staff in all environments, respect is lacking and a source of discontent. The severity of the issue is evident.

It is also clear that the job market in health care simply cannot afford to lose employees, especially over an issue that is easily and inexpensively resolved. The current workforce will simply not tolerate a disrespectful work environment, particularly the most talented workers. It has been demonstrated that employees will determine if they are going to stay or leave based on their relationship with their supervisor or boss. Inarguably, a positive supervisor/boss and worker relationship is based on mutual respect.

Conversely, it is difficult to expect staff to respect residents, families and other visitors in a facility if they themselves are not respected. Staff at all levels wants to be respected. They want to be respected by their boss, supervisors, peers, physicians, administration, residents and families. Not unlike individuals in any field in any position, all desire respect for their personhood and contributions. In fact, individuals often seek and involve themselves in jobs and organizations in which they feel respected. Staff is undoubtedly the link to a successful facility. Without good staff the facility will suffer. All staff, in all departments, should be treated as the important commodity that they are.

Establishing Respect as A Core Value

It is important to establish respect as a core value within a facility. It should be part of the foundation, the vision and mission, and should encompass all persons involved in the facility. It must be communicated as an expectation for all, from all, and not left to the discretion of the parties involved. This includes all staff regardless of their title or position. By necessity, this requires communicating the expectation to not only staff, but also to families and residents.

Respect is established by demanding it for yourself and all of those on staff. The leader will serve to model this behavior in their interactions. If the leader is not respectful to the staff, families and other customers, the staff will see this and do the same. Leaders must first demand it of themselves and practice it daily. It is not acceptable to demean a particular staff person to another or a family member or the corporation. Similarly, it is also not acceptable for managers to be disrespectful. Managers, like the leader, are being watched and evaluated constantly. The staff will model what they see.

Respect is paramount in the interactions with and on the part of families, as well. It is expected that staff is respectful towards residents and families. However, while quick to reprimand staff who are disrespectful towards families, we often overlook the need for families to be respectful toward staff. There are times when families may be respectful of administration and management but fail to treat direct care staff in a similar manner. It is important to listen to staff and determine what is truly happening. If in fact a family is not being respectful toward the staff, the leader must intervene and educate the family. If the situation does not change, the family must be asked to leave. It is not satisfactory for families to mistreat the employees. Although it may be upsetting to families to be confronted, one needs to do so in a private, tactful manner. In the end, the families will respect the leader for this and so will the staff. The word will spread very quickly among staff that they are being protected and valued.

Conducting Business in Private

When discussing confidential information, a sensitive matter or a corrective action, it is imperative that it is conducted in a private area. Sensitive information should never be discussed in a public space for others to hear. Whether it is an irate family or an out of control staff person, the matter should be taken to a private space to allow for venting and elaboration. No matter how upset or angry the parties are, all ranking staff should know that the expectation is that such matters are discussed in private.

All too often, especially when dealing with a staff problem, managers and administration discuss and sometimes yell or argue with a staff person in front of their peers. It is devastating to the staff person and to the morale of the entire staff. If the leader conducts himself in that fashion with one staff person, others will believe that it may happen to them as well. It is imperative that the respect and dignity of others are maintained by the leader. This provides an invaluable opportunity to teach others how to handle conflict and confrontation while exercising self-control and caring in a difficult situation.

Maintaining Fair and Consistent Practices

Fair and consistent practices serve to benefit all in the facility. Staff should know that policies and procedures are going to be carried out despite an individual's position within the facility. No one person on staff deserves to be treated differently than another. This can be accomplished at the same time that the leader allows for the examination of all situations individually. Fair and consistent does not always mean doing exactly the same thing for every person. It does mean treating people the same when the circumstances are equal. Each individual deserves the opportunity to be individually represented and considered.

Take time to evaluate each situation and talk with all parties involved. Get a total picture of an event or situation so that you can make a truly informed decision. Staff will feel respected and valued when they are heard and treated with fairness.

Recognizing and Celebrating Accomplishments, Contributions and Successes

Respect is looking for and acting upon opportunities to recognize and reward staff. Simply thanking them is a way to start. Recognize them in public and in the presence of colleagues and families. When prospective families tour the facility, take time to introduce them to the staff and give staff credit for their talents. There are infinite numbers of ways to reward and celebrate with staff. Recognition does not have to cost money. More importantly, as indicated by many employees, staff values being acknowledged for an initiative or a task done well. Simply thanking someone for a job well done is often enough.

There are as many recognition strategies as there are tasks. Verbal acknowledgement, personal notes, or recognition in a group or meeting are a few simple ways to celebrate the accomplishment and contribution. In some facilities small tokens or gifts are given. Donuts and other foods are appreciated by the entire staff, as are lottery tickets and gift certificates. Staff will also appreciate efforts to recognize them personally. Birthdays might be acknowledged with a card sent to their homes or a small cake. Holiday cards can be sent to the homes of all staff. Ask the staff for ideas or ways in which they would like to be recognized, in addition to ways they would like to do so for their colleagues.

One of the most effective ways to demonstrate respect is for leaders to give credit to others. This leadership model is a collective effort, where all people make contributions to the end product. As the opportunity arises to receive compliments or awards, leaders should always give credit and recognition to others. This in turn serves to encourage staff to contribute more and achieve. It also serves to increase self worth and satisfaction in work and one's job. Retention is ultimately enhanced. When one is secure as a person, self-recognition is not important. The leader will know in his or her heart that any success is something 'we' have accomplished.
It is important to seek community or public recognition opportunities for the staff and to capitalize on them.

Seek out and apply for any award opportunities in the community. In many cases colleges and community organizations seek to recognize outstanding nurses. Nursing assistant recognition programs exist and serve as an opportunity to highlight exceptional performance. State and national organizations often solicit nominations for awards in all disciplines in long-term care. It takes little time and effort to be involved, and staff deserve this recognition. These are opportunities to get all of the staff involved not only in the selection process, but in the subsequent celebration, as well. It is a major boost to staff just to be nominated. For those who win, it is often a once-in-a-lifetime event. There is nothing more powerful than to see a fellow coworker recognized and receive an award.

Conduct parties; invite staff to celebrate with the award winner. Enable and encourage staff to attend the award ceremonies of their colleagues. Put up banners announcing awards along with pictures and display boards for all of the employees to see and residents and families as well.

Once established, a respectful environment will help to facilitate a team effort, allowing individuals to bring forth their talents and contributions to the enhancement of the entire facility. A foundation of respect helps to facilitate the building of an organization and the trust necessary to work towards a common destination or vision.

 FREQUENTLY ASKED QUESTIONS

How do I begin to establish respect as a core value?

You first begin with yourself. Examine your own feelings about your staff, managers, colleagues, families, customers and others. Do you respect and value them? If not, why? Should you continue to employ them, work with them, or work for them? You need to spend some time thinking about what respect means to you and how that concept should be integrated into the operation and culture of your organization.

Talk with your managers about respect. Ask them to define it, thinking about how they can better apply it in the work place. What specifically can they do to encourage consistent, respectful behavior?

Then discuss it with staff. Make it a topic for an in-service. Ask staff to define what respect means to them and how it should be applied when dealing with residents, families, peers and managers and supervisors. Use specific case examples and work through problem areas with your staff.

Following the initial in-service, respect should remain a topic to be revisited periodically. Staff often loses sight of it in the midst of the day-to-day business of the organization. It is important to keep it fresh in the minds of all staff. Respect should be discussed at least annually, perhaps in the midst of another topic such as the vision/mission or teamwork, or related to a specific incident or problem in the facility.

Finally, demand it. When disrespectful behavior is brought to your attention do not ignore it. Deal with it by citing disrespect as the primary issue and the situation around it as secondary. It is often an issue of making people more aware of their behavior and the impact of that behavior on others; a symptom of an underlying problem rather than an isolated incident.

What do I do if a manager is disrespectful towards staff?

Once you have investigated the situation and found it to be truthful, then you need to take immediate action. You educate the manager and indicate that the power of their position has nothing to do with their right to treat others disrespectfully. It has everything to do with their *responsibility* to promote a respectful workplace. Let them know that you will not allow actions of this kind on their part or any other persons.

While this may be difficult for some managers, in the long run it will serve them, you and the organization. You cannot afford to have a disrespectful manager chasing off employees. However, remember that managers need recognition and positive feedback for the work that they do. As managers work with the leader to recognize staff, they need to know that they are appreciated as well. Be certain to praise their work and reward them for contribution and achievement.

What if I have a family member who is being disrespectful towards staff?

You would not allow a staff person to be disrespectful to a family and thus should not allow a family member to demean staff either. As in all of the other situations that may take place you need to investigate and gather the facts. If indeed a family is being disrespectful, you must deal with it and act as the protector of your staff.

Ask for a meeting with the family and explore their experience with your facility and staff. Then discuss the occurrence with them. Let them know that respect for all is a core value of your facility and that it includes actions with the staff. If the disrespectful behavior continues, you may have to ask the family to leave. While losing a resident is a concern, it could be more costly for you in the long run to allow the behavior to continue, resulting in adverse effects on staff morale and loss of staff. This communicates to families that respect is valued for all in the facility, that you value quality staff, and ultimately quality care for their loved-one.

VISION

Creating a total picture of what you dream of
developing including guiding principals and values.

- Doing what you believe in and value with passion and commitment.

- Creating a vision, mission and philosophy; being the best.

- Establishing guiding principles and values.

- Looking at the whole vs. a part, essentially systems thinking.

- Planning long term and short term vs. reacting to daily crisis.

- Keeping the vision alive.

Kate

Kate attended a business seminar on leadership.   Participants represented a variety of industries, including health care.   Discussion topics included vision and mission, with a strong emphasis on the development of a vision statement.   The vision statement was described as material that should be posted in the building, utilized in marketing, printed on employee business cards, and recited by employees upon request.   While Kate's facility already had an extensive mission statement, with numerous objectives and goals, her organization had not prepared a short statement to use in this manner.   She felt as though she had missed the point of developing a vision.

When Kate returned to the facility, she vowed to work with the staff on developing a catchy and brilliant vision statement that could be used for marketing.   This would be a statement that the staff could learn to say when asked, and one that she would be proud to mount and hang on the walls or put on business cards.

Kate met with staff around the clock; all staff, all shifts, and all departments. She conducted seven separate meetings and encouraged staff to talk about who they were, why they were here, what was important to them in their work, what the organization was trying to achieve. The brainstorming sessions produced a wide-ranging list that including the following characteristics: best individualized care; advocate for residents; dignity and respect for all; homelike environment; clean, safe and secure environment; loving; shoulder to lean on; ear for listening; maximizing individual potential; fun; treating one another like family; involved/intertwined with one another; accepting; supportive; welcoming; patient; individual support; encouraging; dependable; teamwork; knowledge; compassion; facilitators of change; peace; and, troublemakers. Many of these characteristics were repeated over and over by individuals from all departments, in various roles. Kate was so proud and so moved by their love and compassion. It was one of the most incredible experiences Kate indicated she had ever had.

Through this exercise, Kate learned that while the process did not result in a catchy vision statement for business cards or a plaque, the staff did not require one. Staff members had talked about service as so basic to their work, that it had become something unspoken that was valued, believed and lived everyday. While they did develop a vision statement together, they realized that the important result was not in the words but experienced in the actions of special people caring for others. An organization's vision lives in the work and passion of the people who touch the residents, families and friends everyday. Only when the vision is alive, will it truly matter.

Many authors believe that a vision is critical to leadership and serves as a foundation for the purpose, work and success of an organization. While the importance of vision is often recognized, few in health care define it or discuss how to go about establishing a vision for an organization whose unique purpose involves caring for others.

Vision is a total picture of the organization to be created or as it evolves from its existing state. It is what an organization wants to create. It is enhanced by a strong passion for the work and a commitment to the purpose, project or service. "Visioning" involves the creation of a dream organization, thus picturing in one's mind how the organization will look and operate. It involves imagining how it will feel when the vision is achieved. It answers the question, what will the outcome of this vision be on employees, residents, families, and even the community.

In long-term care, visioning means thinking about what kind of facility you want to create. It involves imagining all of the daily operations, all tasks, departments, and personnel. It is envisioning how the facility will look, how staff will appear and feel, and the quality of the relationships and interactions between employees, residents and families. Visioning involves thinking of how people will act, treat one another, and if they look happy and content. It is looking at the whole organization and examining how each and every piece (i.e., staff, departments, programs, environment, policies and procedures) fit and work together.

Why is a vision important? The vision is the ultimate destination for the leader and those who follow. It is the basis for drive and motivation to improve, a desire to be the best. Visioning moves a group of individuals in an organization toward a common destination. If a leader has no vision or destination, how will he know what to do or where he is going? Without vision how does the staff know what to do? Without vision, people just come to work and put in their time. Without a vision, a group of people may come together but go nowhere. Nothing exists that binds them, unites them or excites them.

The Visioning Process

Visioning, and the resulting change that takes place in an organization or facility, is a step-by-step journey. It usually starts with one person or a small group reflecting on what they want the operation or facility to be. Over time, others are invited into the discussion. Consideration is given to factors such as designing particular physical features of the facility, determining the scope and nature of programs and services, establishing the tone and order of daily operations, and confirming standards for the quality of personal interactions. Those involved in the visioning process reflect on all aspects of the operation and what they want it to be. Visioning is the process of thinking, reflecting and brainstorming, in which all are given the opportunity to dream about what will be created. It is rather like collective daydreaming.

By necessity, the vision is guided by a set of fundamental principles and values, such as respect, dignity, trust, honesty and integrity. The vision of a healthy organization will include concepts such as striving to be the best, always evolving, changing and improving. The vision or vision statement is then put into operation by the mission and a set of goals and objectives for the organization. Too often facilities focus on only part of the desired outcomes; usually financial. They rarely consider the needs and issues of residents, families, employees, consumers, and community. Visioning for successful leaders and organizations includes more than financial success.

Once established, the vision is used to lead the organization and provide the basis for decision-making at all levels. Thus, it is actually used in the day-to-day operations of the facility. In one such instance, staff had input into how to solve the problem of weekend absenteeism. They talked with one another and reminded each other of the vision, the commitment to the residents and each other. They established a practice that was fairly simple: any employee who called in absent any particular weekend would automatically be scheduled to work the next weekend. In addition, staff insisted that the administration strictly support the absenteeism policy, even if doing so meant losing some employees. Utilizing the vision in this manner helped staff understand the impact of attendance behavior, and gave them an opportunity to participate in the solution.

Sharing the Vision

The importance of sharing the visioning process and the organizational vision with all levels of staff cannot be overemphasized. While time-consuming, the process of sharing the vision allows not only the contribution and inclusion of others, but aids in building consensus and acceptance of the organization's purpose and direction.

When the vision is relatively clear for the leader, it is time to impart it to others and solicit the input, values and views of others. The leader might decide to first explore the vision with one or two members of the management staff. The next step should be to discuss the vision and examine it with the entire management team. Allowing the management team to brainstorm and contribute to the vision in the early stages provides an opportunity for managers to understand the important nature of the vision in the organization and role model support for the process and resulting implementation.

Once managers have offered input, the vision is shared with all staff, all departments and all shifts, as everyone in the facility has a role to play in acting out the vision and mission in the life of the organization. They need to reflect and examine the proposal. Ask the staff their opinion of the vision. What do they want for their organization? What is important for them to become within the organization?

As you approach the staff with a new vision and way of operating, I have found that the staff has varying levels of commitment. Past experience indicates that staff moves through stages when new cultures or philosophies are instituted. Transformational change takes time, but positive signs can be seen early and all along the way, often in the behavior of the staff. Perhaps this is in part due to the additional time and attention they are paid. Another reason may be that the staff has been waiting for the opportunity and guidance that brings about positive change.

Figure 3 outlines my experience and beliefs about the stages of staff development, acceptance and behavior related to a newly implemented vision in a long-term care facility. Employees arrive and move through these stages at differing rates. Some are slow and some move more quickly. The implementation of the model and the stages of development take time and do not happen overnight. However, improvement in the organization should take place quickly. Improvement in the tone and attitude of some of the staff may be seen almost immediately.

Figure 3.
Stages of Staff Development After Vision Creation

Stage	Staff Behaviors
Non-Believer	• Does nothing except what is required • Offers no feedback, yet is compliant • Does not volunteer to come to meetings and may or may not listen during presentations
Curious	• Attends scheduled meetings • Questions what to do and why • Listens but does not offer feedback
Tester	• Starts to test the system • Tests the administrator/managers to see if actions are consistent with words • May ask for help or come with a problem to see how it will be resolved
Convert/Believer	• Starts to practice what they are learning • Begins to be successful and accomplished • Affects the happiness of someone else, which makes them happy, as well
Committed Believer	• Provides service-oriented care automatically • Takes initiatives to serve, even outside normal work requirements • Does this in the absence of the administrator/manager

Will there be staff who are non-committal or worse, disruptive in this process? Yes, probably. It will take time and commitment to the new vision on the part of the leader to convince them. If, over a long period of time a person or two remains disruptive, counterproductive or cannot support the vision, you might suggest that they should think about working elsewhere. If they are not going to leave, yet continue to be a problem, then treat them as any other problem employee you might encounter. Work them through your disciplinary process and if necessary, terminate them. The work will be hard enough without having someone pulling you and your staff back down. You may find this poor attitude in a manager as well. The same goes for them, as they will hurt and impede your progress.

Creating the Vision by Example

Leaders need to take the time to envision what they want their facilities to be. It takes time and quiet reflection. It is not done in the midst of the day-to-day activities. If leaders don't know what they want the organizational experience to be, no one else will. If the leader is unclear about a destination, what they are working toward, how can the staff be led?

In the creation of the vision, it is critical to think, read about and explore exemplary environments. Talk with successful administrators and other leaders to establish a vision and plan for your facility. This information can be found in the long-term care and gerontology literature as well as the business literature and through professional organizations. Once the leader is clear about their own vision, they need to share and explore the vision with others. As mentioned previously, the input of management and direct care staff is invaluable to the process of creating a vision.

Vision for the Residents

One place to start is to examine what kind of experience you want for the residents. Is an individualized resident program part of the vision? What physical structures and atmosphere do you want to design for the residents? What will the programs and activities include?

Individualized Care

Each person is unique with an equally unique set of needs. The limitations of the health care environment related to staffing and reimbursement often hamper caregivers' abilities to address the diverse physical, social and emotional needs of our residents. When caring for a group of individuals, is it still possible to meet each person's individual needs? My experience tells me that although it takes more time and effort, it is possible. In the long run, it will save time and result in more satisfied residents, families and staff. When an individual's needs are met, that person is happier, creating fewer demands and problems within the facility and for the staff.

This approach is best accomplished by gathering detailed information about the resident and examining that information for clues to meeting individual needs. The resident and their family are valuable resources in this process. For instance, gather information on sleep and eating patterns. Perhaps an individual liked to sleep later in the morning and have a light breakfast. In such a case, that person should be allowed to sleep until waking and a continental breakfast served to them. While this appears to take more staff time, it does not. Dealing all day long with the behaviors of someone who did not get the amount rest to which they are accustomed is far more problematic and time-consuming for staff than allowing residents to sleep late and providing an individual breakfast from the kitchen.

Although it will not be possible to meet each person's individual needs at all times, solutions are often very simple and easily addressed when flexibility and creativity are employed and encouraged. Staff must learn how to balance the needs of one person with the needs of the group. Experience, as well, teaches staff how to plan for each individual rather than the group, later linking like individual needs with group solutions.

Physical Environment

Making alterations in the physical environment is a wonderful place to start enacting a vision. Staff, residents and families can see the vision as tangible as it unfolds in the physical changes you make. What do you desire in the physical environment you provide for staff, residents and families? Is it important to provide an attractive, comfortable and clean environment? Whatever type of environment you decide to create, you need to be clear about it and then set about making it happen. Engage others in the process of making the physical environment consistent with the vision of the organization.

For instance, you may decide that you desire an environment that is more residential in appearance. As such, each room in the facility should contain furniture and items that one might find in a home.   Residents' bedrooms would be different, capitalizing on items they bring from their own home. Discuss this with staff and encourage them to think in this fashion. Implement the philosophy that if it is not an item typically found in a home, it will not be part of the residential facility environment.

Emotional Atmosphere

The emotional environment is equally important.   It is something that has to be created and controlled. It does not just 'happen.'   Too much noise and commotion are uncomfortable and can escalate anxiety for residents.   A hostile or negative emotional atmosphere for staff can set up a situation that breeds dissatisfaction, unwanted attendance behaviors and effects on the quality of care for residents.   Likewise, staff attitudes and emotional treatment of families can increase family stress related to nursing home placement, lead to family dissatisfaction with care, census problems and an unfavorable reputation in the community.   Recognizing and solving problems with the emotional atmosphere of care can affect quality and satisfaction problems associated with the physical environment.   The vision of the organization must then include concrete consideration to not only how the facility looks and smells, but also how it feels.

For example, when caring with persons affected by dementia, staff may value a calm emotional atmosphere that contributes to decreased levels of agitation and anxiety among residents.   Decreasing the amount of noise and activity serves to keep residents calmer and focused on the task at hand. Establishing a calm environment means establishing expectations and educating staff about the effects of the environment on residents, particularly with regard to noise and other forms of stimulation.   Encourage staff to talk quietly, not yell, when speaking to one another on the units. It is also helpful to move about in a quiet and relaxed manner.   Noise can be reduced by limiting the use of the intercom, music or by turning off televisions and radios, unless being used therapeutically.

The atmosphere must not be left to chance, but must be purposefully designed and maintained.   It requires a concerted effort to identify and establish such an atmosphere, as well as the involvement of everyone in order to maintain it.   It also requires time and continuing effort.   As with other aspects of the vision, ongoing discussions with all staff and purposeful reminders about the emotional atmosphere of the facility, whether formal or informal, benefit the residents, families and staff.

Activity Programming

What happens during the course of the day for many long-term care residents rests in the leader's hands.   The leaders determine how much or how little is invested in this department.   Activity programming that is either too advanced or too boring is a source of behavioral problems in long-term care.   As with other care programs related to individual needs and preferences, activity programming that provides one activity for a diverse population day in and day out will fail.   There will be some activities that some of the residents like to do and some that they either do not enjoy or cannot accomplish.   The key is to find activities that each person enjoys and to offer multiple events for residents with varied abilities.

In addition, activities need to be conducted inside and outside of the facility. Programs could take place on the facility grounds and may include something as simple as a picnic or a walk.   Getting residents outside lifts their spirits, gives them variety and offers things to focus on other than the same four walls.   Trips and outings are very enjoyable for all residents, even those with dementia.   Shopping trips, going out to lunch, to the theatre or the zoo serve to be a source of joy for residents.   Even something as simple as a ride and ice cream can make a major difference.   The memory and feelings of experiencing life outside the facility remain with the residents, even those with dementia.   The only requirements are creativity, careful planning and a commitment to providing such programs.

What do you want the activity program to accomplish?   What is your commitment to the department and their programs?   How can they bring quality to the lives of the residents?   What kind of activities do you envision for your residents?   Does one activity serve all of the residents or even most of them?   Is there a way to provide multiple activities to better meet the needs of all residents? The visioning process provides a unique opportunity to examine all the possibilities open to your facility and those for whom you care.

Vision for Families

While it is true that residents come to us as unique individuals, they also come with equally unique families and familial relationships. Family involvement, needs and experience must also be considered in the vision for your organization.   How will you assist and accommodate families? What are their expectations of you, the staff and the facility?   What would you expect were you in their position? What do you want from families?   Vision needs to include your commitment and focus on programs for, and approaches to families. Families are very much a part of many facilities' daily lives. Many family members visit each and everyday, and become friends with staff, other residents and families. They are often people the staff cares deeply about. In a way, the facility's staff becomes an extension of the family.

Family Accommodation

Creating a positive family experience requires effort and planning, beginnings with the first phone call. How will the calls that come in from prospective residents' families be handled? Do you have an automated system or menu that a caller must find their way through in order to talk with a real live person and once a caller gets a person on the phone, how will they be treated?

It is important to understand that calling a long-term care facility for services is a very difficult step for families. It often takes families weeks or months to finally decide that they can no longer provide the care their loved ones' need. They often feel sad, distraught and guilty. They may pick up the phone and dial several times before they actually have the courage to talk to someone. How do you think they will feel when they find they must wade through a maze of phone options? They may hang up and may not call again.

The same will happen if they have to wait or if the person answering the phone is distracted or unpleasant. I think in many cases you only have one chance to attract a family to your facility and the first opportunity is usually over the phone. At that point, if you lose the family, you will no doubt lose them forever. Although it is difficult to measure, the responsiveness of your facility to prospective families also becomes part of your reputation in the community.

Once a family visits your facility to tour, how will they be greeted and treated? What will they smell, hear and see? What kind of interactions will they experience with your staff or observe between staff and residents? This speaks volumes to families. If they are mistreated when they are touring, a time when you should look your best, they will surmise that other contacts will be less than perfect including the care of their loved ones.

I visit a lot of long-term care facilities, and on many occasions, I've been poorly impressed from the outset. Despite the presence of staff members in the vicinity, I have often found them occupied - talking on the phone or otherwise ignoring me as best they could. At one facility, two staff people were sitting in the reception area, talking with each other and looking at magazines. Neither looked at me nor spoke to me until I asked them a question.

Is your vision to accommodate families upon request or will you have fixed hours that you will accept them? Will phone calls be answered only for specific hours out of the day? Will the tours be limited to 9-5, Monday through Friday? If the admissions director is not available, will someone else be prepared to work with a call or tour?

Families need help and information when they need it or have time for receiving it. Family needs don't occur conveniently between the hours of 9 and 5, Monday through Friday. A system can be established where staff is available when families require or request help. Staff can be paged when a phone inquiry or request for information comes in, regardless of when the request occurs. The administrator or management staff needs to be available to handle all phone calls from families in the evenings or on weekends. Receptionists can be trained to secure a name and phone number and then page the person on-call. Calls can be returned and needs addressed when they arise. Such responsiveness is a hallmark of a facility where families are important to the vision of the organization. Families will feel that they matter when you are available and interested in their needs and concerns.

Family Involvement

Once the family has made the decision to place their loved one in your facility, what level of family involvement do you envision? Will you encourage family involvement and participation in care and facility activities? Will staff engage the family as part of the care team toward keeping the family relationship intact? Are there structural mechanisms for communicating and staying in touch with families that you would like to put in place or expand?

Events such as family meetings, educational programs, dinners and socials can be marvelous ways to engage families. These encourage family interest and involvement, and serve as opportunities to keep in touch with families and their needs. They also give families something to do and focus upon during their visits with residents, which may otherwise seem awkward or foreign to them. Spending social time together also enhances staff and family relationships. Finally, participation in the life of the facility provides a sense of belonging and comfort as families become acquainted with other families who share their experience. The more involved a family is in the activities and care of their loved one, the more they feel a sense of empowerment, belonging and value, the more satisfied they will be with the facility and care.

Guiding Values and Principles

Guiding principles and values are the ways in which an organization conducts work on a daily basis. Important to the vision are the principles and values that are embraced, implemented and conveyed to the staff. Honesty, integrity and trust are essential components of working with people, and guide the operations and personal interactions within the organization.

I have observed administrators whose actions reflect an attitude that staff is not very smart or can somehow be fooled. Direct-care staff may not often have the educational level of the administrator, but to assume that they are not intelligent or can be easily fooled is in itself a foolish assumption. Staff members know when someone is sincere and when they are not. Sincerity is evident in nonverbal attitudes and actions, and the everyday treatment of staff. For instance, successful leaders don't ask people for their opinion if those opinions are not valued. While this strategy may work in the short term, it will be devastating to the health of the organization in the long run. If and when the staff find out the leader is insincere, they will not believe or trust again.

Being open and honest involves meaning what you say and saying what you mean. It is more than just telling the truth. It also involves a willingness to admit that one is wrong; wrong in a decision about staff, an approach to a resident or perhaps a situation with handling a family concern. Everyone makes mistakes. Staff and families are much more understanding and forgiving when an undesirable event or situation is discussed honestly and mistakes are admitted openly.

Integrity is not only meaning what you say but also following through. If staff cannot trust the administrator or what he or she says, administrators will not be able to lead.   Employees simply will not follow.   Leaders who make a commitment to do something must do it, no matter how busy or what other events occur in the process.   Leaders should not promise things that they cannot, or do not intend to deliver.

Trust is essential in order to get the best from people.   Trust is the foundation for relationship development critical for leadership.   Trust, like respect and caring, is a choice.   If the leader chooses not to trust or is not trustworthy, then the team will not develop and the vision will be unrealized. Trust starts with the leader.   The people who are asked to follow will not trust the leader until the leader earns and returns trust.

Looking at the Whole Organization and Long-Term Thinking

Visioning and the implementation of the vision is a process. The creation of a new facility or the development of a different culture is a long-term project. With this in mind, facilities must look at the long term, rather than just focusing on the short term, or managing the crisis of the day.   While crises must be managed, solving them must not to be the only goal.   A crisis orientation will stifle the development of future goals and programs by keeping the leader distracted and unfocused.

Focusing on the vision and the future for the organization means considering the impact of all plans, programs and decision, internally and externally, and over time.   Even the simplest decisions may have an impact on multiple people and departments. (e.g., holding a party for nursing staff to the exclusion of other departments)   Before making a decision, think about whether it supports the vision of the organization including its effect on all parties involved.   While an administrator may not see the total outcome of a decision for some time, potential outcomes for the whole organization and its components need to be considered.

This requires reflection on the problem or program, gathering relevant information, and considering possible actions.   For example, if a large number of staff members are leaving, the administrator must find out why instead of just hiring another person and filling the vacancy.   Leaders gather information from the staff members who are leaving.   Record and examine the results to identify any trends or systematic problems related to turnover. Once the information is generated, administrators have to take action.   If one or more issues seem to be causing turnover, it is critical to implement measures that keep that situation from happening again. Perhaps several individuals report that a specific supervisor has mistreated them. Such behavior must be investigated, tracked and dealt with. Identify what the supervisor is doing to chase people away and correct it. It may simply be a need to educate the supervisor and to be clear about the way he/she is expected to treat others. If it is not dealt with, the supervisor will continue to contribute to problems with staff retention. Continue to monitor the situation to be certain the intervention was effective.

Keeping the Vision Alive

Success comes from creating and then keeping the vision alive. The vision needs to be used frequently to remind people about why they are there, what they are working toward, and how they will accomplish common goals. First, it should be utilized in the interview process for all prospective employees to ensure that you are hiring people who can become contributing members of your organization. The vision and mission must then be reviewed and updated with all staff at least once a year and any other time the staff needs to be focused, motivated or redirected.

Creating a vision that is shared by the staff takes time and effort. It also takes time and effort to keep the vision alive. It does not happen on its own. The vision and mission must be discussed and examined routinely for as long as the organization is operational. Continually talk about it in meetings and as problems and issues arise. This will enhance the vision and make it part of the driving force for all decisions that are made. The process begins with the leader who models its importance and uses it in decision-making. Others witness as the vision drives a leader's motives and actions.

FREQUENTLY ASKED QUESTIONS

My building is already operating. How do I institute a vision now?

Everyday is a new day and can be a new start. You follow the same process addressed in defining service for your facility. First you develop a vision of your own. Then engage others in the process until you have a complete and consistent vision.

How do I create a vision for my facility?

You need to think about your organization and what you want it to be – your dream of the organization. Spend time, several sessions, to think and reflect on what you want to become with no restrictions. Just dream. It is helpful to find another person to discuss this with a colleague, mentor or friend. Once you have a solid idea of what you want, you can involve others in the process. To facilitate a collaborative vision, discuss your vision with management and ask for their input and then discuss with all staff and ask for their input. Together, you create a vision that is shared by all staff.

While this may be difficult and time consuming, especially for large organizations, it is important. It may simply take longer. Even in large facilities and organizations, staff need to have an idea about the purpose in their work and what the organization is dreaming of becoming.

I work in a corporation and they gave me our corporate vision. How do I work with this?

While the corporate vision must often be adopted, there is no reason to expect a vision to be applied uniformly from one facility to the next. With the input of staff, take the vision statement one step further by deciding how that vision will be implemented in your unique facility with residents, families and staff. Discuss how it will guide and impact *your* particular facility. Staff can be very creative and motivated by a simple statement of purpose when they are given the freedom to dream beyond it to actual care and activities. So meet with the staff and ask them: How will we make this vision work for us and those we serve?

I have so many crises everyday. How can I possibly plan long term?

If you never have a plan for where you are going, you will do nothing but handle the crisis of the day, everyday. While problems or situations occur on a daily basis in every industry or business, you will go nowhere without a vision and plan for getting there. It's quite likely that a well-functioning vision will help reduce the number of crises and bring some stability to the facility.

Won't the staff think I am crazy sharing a vision, a dream for the facility? Will they laugh at me?

No. They will be interested. They, too, need to find meaning in their work, to make a difference and to know where they are headed. Most employees will work better with a vision – a destination in mind, something to work towards. Creating a vision with individuals in an organization can be a wonderful experience. The challenge for leaders is keeping the vision alive in the day-to-day operations of a facility.

INCLUSION

**Involving everyone as a partner in the evolution
and progression of the project.**

- Respecting, appreciating and recognizing the input and contributions of others.

- Staying connected to staff.

- Seeking the right persons and trusting them.

- Communicating expectations and requiring accountability.

- Adopting a flat organizational chart philosophy.

- Listening, supporting and teaching.

- Recognizing and celebrating accomplishments.

- Promoting dialogue, formal and informal, honest and open.

Staff as Part of the Solution

A facility was experiencing a great deal of rapid staff turnover. New employees were not staying very long; only a few weeks. In a meeting discussing the concern with all staff, multiple strategies were offered by employees to decrease the quick turnover. A tour of the entire facility during the interview process was suggested as a way to enable prospective workers to see all work situations and environments. Existing employees also discussed ways to welcome new staff members to the facility, and what a welcoming attitude could accomplish. All employees were encouraged to introduce themselves and include new staff members in work and break times. Optimistic, energetic staff were also identified for mentoring new staff. Anyone who did not want to be a mentor did not have to accept that role. New employees were surveyed at two weeks following hire about their work experience and feelings to determine deficiencies. These initiatives and others decreased the rapid turnover.

Planning a new project

One facility received approval to develop and build an outdoor garden for its residents. Staff had been requesting a garden for some time because taking residents outside seemed so positive. The staff members also wanted more access for all residents and additional items for the residents to enjoy. A landscape architect was hired, and after talking with some of the administration and management staff, the architect designed the perfect garden.

It was the practice of this facility to gather input from staff on projects, especially major ones such as this. In addition, since this garden had been a staff request, it was important to include them in the planning and design. Staff members were invited to meetings to look at the drawings and make suggestions.

The staff had major concerns about the safety and security of the garden as well as the toxicity of the plants that were planned. It turns out that their modifications also decreased the cost of the garden. Because they knew the residents so well, the staff members anticipated the residents' reaction and behavior in the garden. The changes were made to reflect their concerns. Several years later, the garden is a great source of pleasure and comfort for the residents and families. It is also used a great deal by the staff who bring the residents outside to enjoy the garden that they designed. A potentially dangerous and costly mistake was avoided by communicating with the staff on this project.

Today, individuals expect more from their jobs than ever before. They want to be involved in something meaningful. They want to make a difference. They want to know that what they are doing matters in life. In addition, they want to be a part of a group or team who work together to achieve a goal. They want to participate in the organization, be valued for their contribution, and to know that they are doing a good job.

While these expectations seem to be very basic to human nature and even logical, that is not what staff frequently find in health care and long-term care today. Often there is little communication, with no universal discussion of plans, problems or ideas. In many environments, employees simply come to work doing his or her individual thing, with little or no hope of impact or being included in decisions that affect their work or work environment. Why shouldn't everyone have a voice and be included in the operations and plans of a facility?

Inclusiveness has been indicated specifically as a characteristic that leaders must have to be successful. An inclusive environment is one in which all individuals are valued, appreciated, invited and encouraged to participate in the evolution of the vision, mission and development of the project. The leader seeks the right person for the job, communicates needs and expectations, and then trusts the person to do that job, while enforcing accountability for the work. This type of leader recognizes that everyone is valuable to the organization. It is the forging of a partnership, accepting that everyone is in this together and needs each other to be successful.

The foundation of mutual inclusion is trust - the ability to get beyond game playing and have true and meaningful dialogue that is both honest and open, whether formal or informal. With that trust comes the ability to listen to ideas and concerns, with respect and appreciation, and recognize the contribution of others. This leadership model embraces the need for inclusion of all parties involved in the operation of the facility.

Respecting and Recognizing the Input of Others

Residents

The inclusion of the residents and their opinions, whether voiced or determined through their behavior, should be at the heart of how the facility operates. Every decision should be made to satisfy the needs of those entrusted to our care. There are unlimited ways to include residents in the decision-making process. Some are as simple as asking for resident input directly by the formation and active role of resident councils and advisors to staff committees. Satisfaction surveys can be used to periodically keep in touch with how residents view the physical environment and services of the facility, how they feel about interpersonal relationships and care provided by staff, and what they would like to see in the way of improving their experience as residents.

Families

Resident families have a great deal to offer as well. Families hold valuable information about the resident. Families know the resident's history, what they like, what motivates them and what upsets them. This information enhances the staff's ability to work with the residents, meet needs and ensure quality in a resident's life. It is important to stay open to their comments and suggestions, even when they are painful to hear.

There are a variety of ways to include families. Routine family meetings are one way. Monthly family meetings serve as a means of educating families, informing them about events and changes in the facility, and provide an opportunity to secure their input. Family meetings also are venues for determining or soliciting family questions and concerns that can be addressed proactively, alleviating future problems and enhancing satisfaction. One-on-one meetings also keep one in touch with family needs for support. Just as it is important to actively include residents on councils and committees, family councils and participation in decision-making for the organization provide a wealth of creative ideas and thoughtful suggestions for improving the environment and care. Knowing your families and their level of motivation to be part of the process is valuable to the leader's success. Families are not only customers, but can also be resources in the development and implementation of the vision.

Similarly, periodic family surveys, conducted on an anonymous basis, can provide very candid and honest evaluations of care, environment, staff and services. However, don't ask if you don't want to know or have no intention of addressing their comments. Like other stakeholders in the vision, families want to be heard and will expect reasonable response in the form of observable or communicated change. Again, look at family satisfaction surveys as an opportunity to measure success and their responses as a resource for improving quality of services and care.

Staff

Although wages need to be competitive, what makes staff stay or leave is how they are treated. People are moved more by their heart and soul than their pocketbooks. While many facilities are attempting to secure staff with money and bonuses, employees actually want most to be respected, heard, included and to be a part of the decision-making team.

Staff must be a part of the operations of a facility. Inclusion enhances their interest and participation and gives them a sense of ownership in the operations and facility achievement. It gives them something to work for. It also provides an opportunity to tap their knowledge and experience to improve the facility operations and resident care.

Staff members are open to learning and innovation. They accept it willingly when involved in the planning and implementation process. There seems little that staff will not try as long as they are a part of the discussion and understand the reason to do so. When invested like this, staff members are more committed to solving issues and more content in their work.

Holding routine monthly meetings with all staff to relay information, discuss issues, plan and problem solve models a philosophy of inclusion on the part of the leader. These meetings enhance communication and staff input. They demonstrate to the staff that employees are valued and that leaders are interested in what employees need, think and say. Monthly meetings enhance teamwork and a philosophy that everyone is in this together. Overall, a meeting ensures a more effective organization. A meeting should be held at least once a month for all staff, on all shifts, to communicate and share thoughts and ideas. These meetings need to be held at least twice on each shift, on all three shifts. The purpose of doing so is to include all staff and make it easy and convenient for staff to attend.

Recently, one administrator boasted among a group of colleagues that he had met with his entire staff, all departments, in one afternoon meeting. He was discussing what the staff had to say and all that he learned. He was very excited about this experience, and his progressive action. When asked how often he did this he indicated that it had occurred six months earlier. Despite the positive outcome, he had not met with them since. Like this administrator, many administrators do not tap the resources of their staff members, and lose touch with them and the care they are providing. Even in large and multi-site organizations the leader needs to be in touch with the individuals providing the service.

To facilitate inclusion, it is important for the leader and management to check in with staff on a regular basis. It is difficult for many employees to ask for anything. Question them, probe, and spend some time with them. While many support the concept of 'management by walking around,' this concept of inclusion is more than just walking around. It involves caring about the people you see, including the quality of the work they provide, assessing their needs, and asking how you might help in response. When needs are evident, management and administration should just help without asking staff what they need; the help will be recognized and always appreciated. Helping staff also communicates that you are not asking them to do anything you are not willing to do yourself. Caring about staff means staying connected with them, being genuinely interested in them, spending time in their space, on the units. In essence, be on the floor. Doing so should be an expectation not only for administration but also for all of the management staff. In time, staff will sense genuine concern, a sense of belonging and trust.

In larger organizations, being in touch with staff is no less important than in smaller organizations. Each individual on staff is not included in each meeting or discussion but a representative sample should be. The excuse that a facility or organization is too large or spread out is simply that - an excuse. If businesses can accomplish this task with thousands of employees in multiple settings around the world, so can long-term care environments. Activities that keep managers and the administrator in touch with staff must be scheduled just like meetings are scheduled.

Another important way of including staff is to conduct anonymous staff surveys. Ask staff how they feel about their work environment, work conditions, policies and procedures, relationships with others, including families, residents, peers and supervisors. Do they feel supported, included and cared for? What is important to them in their work? What can be done to improve their work experience? Give staff confidence that they can answer honestly and openly without fear of consequences for negative responses. This is best done by using an independent agent who can compile and summarize information keeping it anonymous to administrators, managers and supervisors.

Administrators and managers will need time to do an analysis of the survey information and then implement interventions for the areas that the staff may have identified as problematic. There must be a willingness on the part of the leader to address the issues that arise. Do staff members believe that all issues will be addressed and resolved? Hardly. But if employees do not see some action, they will not participate and trust in the process. Follow-up meetings serve to remind staff that over the course of time issues are addressed as programs are implemented and change occurs.

Seeking the Right Persons and Trusting Them

In an effort to create the culture you envision it is important to select the right people to fulfill the purpose and mission of the organization. Many facilities are simply filling 'slots,' or 'holes,' giving little attention to the potential employee's background, motivation or desire to work.

Given the current and impending workforce issues, it is imperative that long-term care facilities and organizations change how they hire and retain employees. There is and will continue to be a limited number of individuals for direct care positions. If a facility is going to survive, the leader will need to recruit and hire thoughtfully and embrace an organizational inclusive approach to retaining employees. As noted earlier, it is not money alone that attracts and keeps employees in an organization.

Recruiting and selecting quality staff based upon the vision and needs of the organization must be handled by a process that takes into account a number of characteristics. It should include past work experience and behavior, individual fit with regard to the other staff, residents and families, agreement and acceptance of the organization's vision and mission, an understanding and acceptance of work expectations, and an informed decision to accept the position based upon discussion of and tour of the facility. Role playing may be used to identify individual characteristics that are either desirable or undesirable in a prospective employee. How would they handle an angry or disgruntled family member? What would they do if a resident became combative during personal care? What action would they take when faced with a lazy or negligent colleague? If they saw an unfamiliar visitor wandering in the facility what would they do?

Once an administrator or manager thinks that he/she has the "right person" for the job and prepares the employee for that job, administrators need to trust them to do the job. If an administrator/manager does not trust the employee, the employee will not return trust. Will employees ever do things wrong? Of course they will. It is important that unmet expectations or a bad result is handled from a trust perspective, trusting that staff were well-selected, with reasonable ability, yet remaining human and capable of improvement and behavioral change. If something is not good enough, then find out who is responsible and discuss it with them. This requires a different response than is typical. Give staff the benefit of the doubt and educate them rather than punishing them.

Like all staff, managers also must be prepared, trusted and allowed to make decisions. It is important to listen to managers, give them different perspectives to contemplate, but ultimately let them decide on the appropriate action. If the administrator has selected the right person and prepared him/her well, that manager will make good decisions. Sometimes managers will not make the right decision on their own. Perhaps they did not consider all of the information or options. Administrators should discuss it with them calmly from a teaching perspective, not a punitive one. Examine mistakes and consider them as an opportunity to learn.

Communicating Expectations and Accountability

Encouraging an inclusive atmosphere and building an interdisciplinary team takes communicating the expectations for working together. Leaders who have an expectation that all departments *will* work together and get along need to say so and make it happen. If conflict and uncooperative behavior is allowed to occur, they will. If administrators do not allow departments to fight and poke at one another, then they won't. It is really up to the administrator. Communicate that everyone is valued. It is everyone's job to see that the care and environment is top quality, and they will live it. If the administrator's expectations are low, the result will be poor care and conflict. Leaders must set the standards very high in order to get what they want.

Expectations need to be in force for the managers, as well. They are members of the team and in fact, role models for the rest of the staff. Remember that, if the employees see managers get away with something, they will expect that they can do the same. If an administrator has concerns about what a manager might be doing or not doing, the issue must be addressed directly and quickly. It will not go away. Just one member of the management team can be extremely disruptive and keep a team from working as one. Effective leaders don't keep disruptive managers, especially if they are a negative influence on others, department managers or staff. The negativity will harm the organization and impair progress. Give each employee every chance to succeed, but if there are no changes in the negative behavior or attitudes, let them go.

All members of the team need to know that they have a voice and a place to go when conflicts cannot be resolved. An open door policy can serve to accomplish this goal. Although it need not be unrestricted access, staff members need to know they can count on it. However, the involvement of the administrator must be predicated on the complainant having tried to resolve the issue with the person involved, including the supervisor or manager. Managers should know this, as well. If a staff member has brought an issue to their attention, everyone has the opportunity to take the concern to the next level. Again, it is not a matter of discipline, but one of respect. Managers should know that the employees have the right to be heard, and the right to carry a concern further if not resolved.

It is often effective to bring the two disputing parties together with the mediation of managers or administration. Conflicts should not be ignored, but dealt with directly and privately. Each party should have the opportunity to discuss the situation from their perspective, with the expectation of confidentiality. The administrator or manager serves as the facilitator, re-connecting the two parties and helping them to resolve the issue together in a mutually satisfying way. Most of the time getting each party to examine the situation from the others' perspectives will bring about resolution.

At times, department managers have difficulty working together. The leader should encourage them to work it out together in a respectful fashion and/or get involved to see that the issue is resolved. Employees look to managers as role models. Managers must support one another and manage conflicts with each other effectively and in a way that sets an example for staff.

Adopting a Flat Organizational Chart Philosophy

An organizational chart exists in most facilities with the leader at the top. The leader, the administrator in long-term care, ultimately holds the responsibility for all decisions made in the facility. There are times when the leader must make a decision alone and everyone needs to understand that this is a possibility. To expedite a process or in an emergency or crisis, everyone needs to be clear about who is in charge and responsible.

In this model, the leader adopts a flat organizational chart where no one person is more important than another or favored over another, regardless of role or position. Staff members are asked for their input on issues that affect them in their lives or their work. Those ideas are considered important to the process and vision of the organization, and used for the benefit of the operation. The organization is in essence a partnership.

Staff should receive feedback in a timely manner and be told not only what is going to happen, but also why something may or may not happen. For instance, staff may decide that they want a big-screen television for the living room. It is leadership's responsibility to discuss with them why this is or is not a good idea. The residents in that particular area may be too stimulated by a large television. It may be too expensive at this time. Discussion occurs to inform staff when it may be reasonable to purchase such an item if beneficial for the residents. Staff may have questions about why the health insurance does not have a lower deductible or why they are paying part of the cost of the insurance. Information is gathered and meetings are held to discuss the insurance program, why it was chosen and what it would mean to the staff to change it. These forums serve to demonstrate a commitment to informing all staff and valuing their opinions and reactions.

Listening, Supporting and Teaching

It is widely recognized that effective communication involves an exchange of information, thoughts, and ideas. By necessity, this exchange requires listening. Listening with sincere intent provides crucial information related to the support and education needs of staff, as well as the solutions to problems within the organization. Listening to staff is critical. Administrators must stop what they are doing when staff members want to talk and really hear what they have to say. Encourage managers to do the same. Listen actively. Be present, not thinking about other things, answering the phone or looking around. Ask thoughtful questions for clarification.

The genuine act of listening communicates respect, validates concerns and encourages future exchange. In the listening, administrators will discover information that will enhance their ability to work with staff by exposing work-related or personal issues or events that are affecting their work environment. Administrators will often find that some employees have never had the opportunity to learn how to handle a major life problem or crisis. An employee's typical response to a problem may be to ignore it, run away, or leave the facility. When an employee is acting unusual or seems to be troubled, administrators and managers should have an already established relationship that is supportive enough to ask the employee what is wrong. While some of the staff will not want to talk about their problems, at least they will know that someone cares and will talk when, and if, they are ready.

Staff is often troubled by and require assistance with personal issues. These may include needing someone to care for their children, being behind on their bills, struggling with broken down cars and no money to fix them. In any of these situations, leaders can help by teaching staff not only how to work through a particular situation, but how to keep some of these problems from happening in the future. Some staff react instead of thinking things through. Many simply have never learned life skills or how to plan ahead. For instance, an employee's car broke down and she had no money to fix the car or transportation to get to work. Her solution to the problem was to quit work. After talking with her and helping her to see that this would only compound the problem, we worked with her to get assistance to fix her car so that she could continue to work. Colleagues assisted her with rides to and from work until the car was repaired.

Other stressful incidents will occur within the facility. The administrator needs to be supportive of staff in emotionally difficult times. This requires sensitivity to what the staff may need and the willingness to follow through. Events may include the unexpected death of a resident, an altercation among staff, or a conflict between staff and a family. In one facility, a resident unexpectedly committed suicide in the night. The administrator was called by staff to inform him of the incident. Staff told the administrator that they were all right, so he did nothing. There should be no question here; someone among that staff needed that administrator. In such a situation the administrator should not even ask, they should go to the facility. It should not matter what time of the day or night. Staff members look to the administrator and managers for support and often need to know that the person in charge cares about their well-being. When staff members need support, they need to know that the administrator and managers will come, even in the middle of the night, and often not for anything other than to see that the staff is okay. Don't just tell them - show them.

Listening is rendered meaningless, however, if there is no intent to act on the information. Listening to what staff members want in their work offers an opportunity to address issues in practice. It may relate to specific policies or procedure, staff education needs, or other practical issues of staff job satisfaction. For example, employees may indicate that they want permanent assignments. Staff members often enjoy working with a specific population. Some like working with residents who are independent, where the bulk of the care involves supervision and recreation. Others like to work with the residents who require more physical care. Employees naturally find their place and the population with whom they wish to work. Permanent assignments can increase knowledge and enhance staff relationships with residents and families. As long as the residents are well cared for, the decisions regarding assignments should be left to the staff.

There are situations where staff members think they might enjoy working in another department. As these situations arise, it is important to listen and support these decisions. When properly matched, permit them to do so. For instance, someone in housekeeping may like to become a nursing assistant. As positions become available, be creative in allowing staff to gain experience in another department. It may prove to be that exceptional nursing talent is discovered, having previously gone untapped. Even if the staff is not happy with the change from housekeeping to nursing, a return to housekeeping can provide a more content staff member and one who is more knowledgeable and sensitive to their colleagues in nursing.

Job flexibility is another staff priority, and often more important than benefits or salary. It is a benefit that staff will identify as one of the reasons that they stay in a particular work environment. Flexibility, the ability to work around family events and obligations, matters a great deal to employees. Listen to what is important to staff and be willing to help them even in small ways. Staff will often work together to accommodate individual needs if they become aware that needs exist. The leader is in a position to establish what staff want or need and facilitates creative solutions within procedural boundaries by encouraging teamwork and collegiality.

Managers must also share the leader's commitment to communication and support by listening and taking the time to examine situations from the perspective of staff. Managers and supervisors frequently get so caught up in multiple tasks that need to be accomplished that they may react without thinking or thoroughly investigating a situation. Administrators need to sensitize managers to the effects of that behavior by example and guidance. Ask them key questions that examine the situation from the employee's perspective. How would the manager feel if the administrator were to handle a similar situation or problem in the same manner? What factors contributed to the problem situation? What possible explanations exist for an employee's behavior? What alternative actions could be taken and to what end? Administrators need to help managers step back and look at employee incidents from all perspectives and then act appropriately.

Also remember that effective problem resolution requires training and support. Managers must be trained to be aware of the effect of their reactions to problems or situations relayed to them by staff and approach problems methodically. There may be things that they hear through the rumor mill, or things said in a heated moment. It is critical that ample time is taken to investigate situations thoroughly before coming to a conclusion, and certainly before making any statements or decisions. It is important for managers to talk with all parties involved, gathering all the information. All too often what is initially stated does not turn out to be exactly what happened. Like the administrator, managers should not rush to judgment without taking the time to investigate an incident. Over time, the organization will benefit from a reputation of fairness on the part of the administrator and managerial staff.

Promoting Honest, Open, Formal and Informal Dialogue

Dialogue with Families

Inclusion of families begins during the first encounter.   Families should be clued in to their importance in the life of the resident and to the continued philosophy that they are integral to the process of care.   They must be partners with the staff from the planning of admission throughout the resident's stay.

It is imperative to communicate with families and to give them routine opportunities to be included.   Agenda-driven, monthly family meetings provide time to share information with families about new programs or projects, solve problems, and solicit their input.   It is also an opportunity to educate and bring new information to families.   In addition, family meetings are a great way to learn from families what is going well and for families to air concerns.   It is a forum for sharing, listening and learning.   It is also an opportunity for families to socialize with staff and other families.

Less formal gatherings serve to establish relationships with families, as well. Encourage staff members to spend time with families, particularly those in need.   Educate staff in how to talk with them, listen to them and try to comfort them.   Families should feel that they are part of the team.   As relationships develop with families and trust prevails, staff members become an extension of the resident's family and sometimes an extended family member to all.

Dialogue with Staff

Including staff and encouraging participation in the life of the organization also creates a sense of inclusion.   Staff should be encouraged to offer suggestions for solving problems, not just to put forth the problem for others to solve.   No one should be permitted to air a problem or complaint without having some input into possible solutions.   When dealing with a problem, it is not "my problem."   It is "our problem" and, the proper approach is "how are *we* going to solve it?"   All staff will look at situations differently if they see that they are also responsible for some of the solutions, as well as the ramifications.   They are then more invested in the outcomes.   The solution to a problem might cost a great deal of money.   Instead of just saying no, ask staff members for ideas on where cuts can be made to enable the facility to afford an item or new benefit. This encourages staff to think things through and come up with feasible solutions.

Another way to include staff and secure ideas is to involve them in planning for the next year. Plan for 2008 at the close of 2007. Staff from all departments can brainstorm in multiple meetings and create a wish list for the coming year. Encourage everyone to dream, with no regard for cost or ease of accomplishment. Have them include such things as programs, physical plant changes, new supplies and education. Once the list is generated, place items into categories. This information can be used throughout the year to bring about change. Prior to planning for the next year, accomplishments from the current year can be discussed; perhaps as an annual report to staff. This provides a means of letting the staff know what they have accomplished together and reinforces a sense of teamwork and empowerment.

Dialogue with Management Team

Time and communication with the management team also enhances a consistent message to all staff. Everyone on the management team must believe in and support the vision and mission. They in turn will encourage the staff and involve them. Having management meetings in addition to all facility staff meetings is not an indication that there are two levels of staff. It merely facilitates communication and enhances the message for all staff. Weekly meetings give the management team an opportunity to communicate and support one another. Discussions at those meetings should include new information, individual schedules for the week, who is doing what and who may need help. It is a time to discuss problems, new directions and issues, and for the group to suggest solutions. It should be at the same time, day of the week and location so all managers can plan.

Another helpful strategy for team building and dialogue with management involves the use of half- or full-day retreats. Quarterly retreats should take place off-site, in a quiet, peaceful environment. The site and agenda for the retreat should be conducive to strategic planning, social interaction and sharing progress and concerns. The agenda is developed with the input of all department managers. Topics for discussion may include physical plant needs, educational needs and programs to be developed internally. Managers may wish to plan for special staff events for the next year. Any new program or event should be discussed in detail and specific individuals committed to the task or even

The benefits of retreats extend from the managers to staff. Retreats serve as a time for strategic planning and a time to share in detail how the team is doing, what is going well, and what may need to be improved. It is a time to be together socially, in a relaxed environment. This time also enhances an appreciation for individuals outside one's department or discipline, facilitates conflict resolution and reinforces the organizational vision and mission. Managers return to the facility energized and with renewed appreciation for one another. Everyone benefits.

What can be learned from utilizing an inclusive philosophy is how much farther one can travel collectively than one would have traveled alone. People blossom under such a philosophy; they learn from one another and grow as individuals and as a group. An inclusive atmosphere creates improved programs and services as well as greater satisfaction for all involved - residents, families, staff and community. It enhances staff retention and commitment, because it feels good to identify with and be part of a larger community.

 FREQUENTLY ASKED QUESTIONS

There is so little time in the day. How can I stay connected to staff?

You block out designated time in the day to be on the floor with staff. This is essential, especially during the building phase when you are setting expectations and working together to determine the direction and vision of the facility. Initially it will require a considerable amount of time to connect with staff on all three shifts. Eventually, the amount of time will decrease, as staff members are confident and secure in their role and the direction of the facility.

I am afraid to let my people make decisions without me. How should I handle this?

Then you have either hired the wrong people or not prepared them well enough. You will never get very far carrying the entire facility on your back. At best, it will function but it will never grow. Eventually, you'll burn out. Worse yet, you may burn out and stay, not really caring because you have no energy left to care. You need to select, educate and delegate.

Begin by assessing the strengths and weaknesses of you managers. Where they are weak, and ask yourself whether training and purposeful guidance strengthen performance? What areas of strength are being underutilized? Be realistic, but trust people to rise to well-communicated expectations.

People come to me with issues and problems all of the time. I try to have an open door policy but sometimes I am on the phone, or it rings. How do I handle this?

Certainly, you must have to have private time in which to accomplish your work uninterrupted. You might indicate to staff that unless there is an emergency, a closed door means that you are not to be interrupted until it is opened. At times you may need to work on projects outside of the facility. Just let staff know that they can see you at another time or leave a message and you will arrange a time at their convenience. And then be there.

An important component of creating an "open door" atmosphere is to give staff all your attention when you are with them. This requires eliminating distractions and focusing on the current problem or concern. Ask the receptionist to hold your calls or just ignore the phone. Close your door to others. It is a demonstration of the respect you have for them and a sign that you value this time together.

We don't have much money for staff parties. How can I show them that I appreciate them?

You do it in your approach, attitude and actions everyday. Talk with staff, be with them, listen to them, and get to know them. Money may bring them in but in most cases money alone will not retain them. Time and attention are often the things they want.

In addition, any parties or events that you plan do not have to be expensive. It does not even need to be a party. Bringing in food is something all staff appreciate. Organize a party or event to which the staff can contribute. They want to be included and are sometimes offended when not asked. Plan a luncheon, a taco bar, a baking contest, or any other event that they can take part in.

A leader who wishes to accomplish team-building and inclusion must be committed to the effective exchange of information and ideas. They must not only be effective senders but also effective receivers of thoughts and ideas.

COMMUNICATION

Establishing an environment involving
the active interchange of
ideas and expectations.

- Communicating expectations and information to staff toward increasing responsibility and accountability.

- Remaining open and listening to comments, concerns and suggestions.

- Creating opportunities to dialogue regarding new programs, innovations and solutions.

- Surveying for initiatives to improve work experience and quality of care.

Enabling Communication

The nursing assistant was having personal problems, and her morning was not off to a great start. Staff was behind schedule readying the residents for breakfast. The cook, who had worked hard to prepare and serve a difficult breakfast on time, was upset because some of the residents were not yet in the dining room. The cook made a few sarcastic comments to the nursing assistant, who had a few words for the cook in return. Both were about to reach their "boiling points"... and breakfast was served in tense silence.

The tension was obvious. Neither wanted to discuss the situation initially with the assistant administrator, who gently encouraged both to come with her to the office. Behind closed doors, the nursing assistant and cook began speaking loudly and defensively. Gently guiding the staff members, the assistant administrator facilitated calm communication, encouraging each one to discuss their side of the story, and their feelings. It was then that the nursing assistant disclosed some of her personal difficulties, including an adult child to support and the impending foreclosure on her own home. The cook then shared some of her own similar experiences, and offered suggestions and support.

The cook felt badly that she had rushed to judgment. The nursing assistant felt badly for "snapping" at the cook. The tension dissipated. Both became emotional, apologized, and shared a hug before leaving the office together, laughing and smiling.

When employees are asked to choose what contributes to job satisfaction, the presence or absence of an effective communication system ranks consistently high. While no communication system is perfect, a variety of means for relaying and receiving information are essential to effectively leading the organization in a strategic direction. Such mechanisms must communicate not only the vision and direction of the organization, but how staff members are expected to work, interact, and care for residents and families, as well as what families and residents can expect from the facility. The purpose is to tap into all of the resources, knowledge and talent at the disposal of the organization and thus design and implement the best possible mechanisms, programs and solutions.

Regular, purposeful efforts to communicate with staff promote accountability, awareness of problems and concerns, and dialogue about innovative solutions and programs. While the need for communication would seem to be self-evident, none of the other components of the leadership model are possible without the unimpeded exchange of information, thoughts and ideas. Communication is necessary to establish a service ethic in the organization, develop and obtain acceptance of a vision, define educational and support needs of staff, and implement strategies that contribute to the inclusion and respect of all persons affected by the organization.

Communicating Expectations

Active communication is critical in any organization and it is no less important in long-term care. Communication with all persons, including staff, residents and families, must begin at the first encounter and continue throughout the relationship. Without communication, staff members will not understand their responsibilities nor feel accountable for actions and attitudes unless the organization continually and routinely communicates the expectations for duties and job performance, for the goals and direction of the facility, and for the role of each individual in the vision. Without the interchange of information with families and residents regarding the vision and expectations, the administrator and staff are forced into a reactive stance when problems and misunderstandings arise.   Rather than receiving constructive concerns and suggestions, the administrator receives complaints and criticism.

Communication strategies should be educational and informative, with the realization that the need for communicating will never end.   There will be the need for consistent, regular reinforcement as the organization grows and evolves over time.   Inevitably, unique events, situations and problems will require the interchange of information and solutions.   Without the existence of a plan for the flow of information and decision-making, confusion and dissatisfaction will be the likely consequence, whether for staff, families or residents.

Listening and Remaining Open

All managers and administrators need to stay open and truly listen to staff members.   The challenge is to facilitate the interchange of issues and problems, ideas and solutions.   When staff is not permitted to voice their perspective or are not heard when they do, the organization will suffer. Although it is not always pleasant or easy to hear suggestions or criticism, the ability of employees to express themselves without repercussion or judgment is essential.   The administrator and managers must allow the staff to state how they honestly feel, or the facility will never change, improve and grow.

This practice by necessity requires listening to all views and perspectives. The most successful leaders surround themselves with individuals who challenge their thinking, and who make significant contributions to the direction and progress of the organization.   Be ready to listen and consider a fresh perspective, encourage dialogue with managers and staff, and reward the expression of new ideas and innovative thinking with appreciation and praise.   It does not serve a leader to surround him/herself with those who always agree.   The open, honest exchange of information and thoughts will produce more effective programs and practices, increase staff members' job satisfaction and quality of care.

Creating Formal and Informal Dialogue

In order to hear staff constructively on a consistent basis, you need to establish a means for creating dialogue. Formal and informal mechanisms serve to enhance communication. Create avenues for communication individually and globally. Formal, planned communication could include a communication board or book, e-mails, letters attached to pay checks and those sent to staff homes. Routinely scheduled forums conducted by administration/ leadership should include all staff on all shifts, serving to promote communication and the opportunity to keep staff informed of current issues, actions and future initiatives. When meetings are consistently scheduled, this practice gives staff the expectation that regular forums will occur, allowing them to prepare in advance and save issues for those designated times.

Employee forums can be substituted for one of the weekly in-service programs. Initially, in the establishment of a new facility or transformation of an existing one, forums should be held at least quarterly by leadership. Later, less frequent encounters will be necessary, as long as one is held with every important change or project. This may involve issues such as changes in employee benefits, major renovations, or a new initiative.

Informal communications happen on a day-to-day basis as management and administration make themselves available to staff. Being with the staff provides opportunities to educate, communicate and enhances the ability to grasp how the staff is performing and coping. There is no substitute for time spent with staff and nothing more effective than staying connected with the ongoing operation of the facility.

Surveying Staff

Staff surveys serve to measure employees' satisfaction with their work and working conditions. The surveys should include all aspects of their work and the people with whom they work. It is very helpful to ask direct, specific questions about issues surrounding their work and job satisfaction; from supplies to pay, benefits and promotion, and relationships with others in the work environment including families, medical staff, managers and administration. The surveys need to be anonymous; without anonymity, staff members will not provide honest feedback.

When communication flows readily in all directions, issues and concerns are handled quickly with sufficient amounts of information. This promotes better procedures and projects. Everyone is content when they feel free to communicate and know that they are heard to the benefit of all involved, the residents, families and staff.

 FREQUENTLY ASKED QUESTIONS

There are not enough hours in the day. How am I supposed to communicate everything to everybody?

You aren't. You have to carefully choose what is important to communicate and the best method of doing so. In most situations in long-term care so little is communicated that nobody knows anything until it happens. It is important to look at what systems you can put in place to communicate important information including posting, letters, e-mail, and most important, consistent staff forums.

How can I possibly communicate what is expected of staff in all departments for every situation?

Once you give the staff an opportunity to be a part of the development of the vision and/or explain an already existing vision to them, you are giving them a great deal of information in which to use to make decisions on their own. Initial and ongoing education and training will enable them to make the decisions you desire. Again, they will not always make the same decision you will, but if the organization's vision is consistently communicated to them, their decision should be appropriate. Change will not happen overnight - they need to thoroughly understand the direction and vision for the facility. Staff will look to you – the decisions you make and how you operate – to get a handle on your commitment to the vision.

It is impossible to anticipate the hundreds of situations that will occur in which employees will have to make a decision. Use the routine staff meetings and forums to communicate to staff that which has gone well and those situations in which there was a problem. Use these examples as a means of teaching them an alternative way for the future.

I am expanding my corporation, with new locations. How can I communicate these expectations in all locations as one time?

A common mistake in business expansion is using multiple sites as an excuse for failure. Blaming the expansion and size on the lack of quality or communication is common. Again, what is important is building the foundation for each and every location. It is not unlike the foundation you built for the first facility; expansion, in fact, should be easier because many systems are already in place. Look again to the SERVICE model and implement each program from the existing facility into the next location. First define and discuss service and whom you are to serve. As a collective group, determine your destination as an organization - the vision. Set up a routine education and communication/support program. Establish respect as a core value and communicate the expectation. Create an inclusive environment for building and sustaining your facility. Make certain to take care of yourself and others in the process.

Understand that each environment will be slightly different and the staff will determine some of those differences. Bring in the appropriate existing systems once the vision, mission and goals are established. Those are what will drive the staff and organization to the destination you have in mind.

A leader needs to be individually prepared to transform a business or organization. Leaders need to be committed, honest with themselves, to know who they are and where they are headed in order to lead others. They must seek and be open to new information and learning as a life-long journey. The next chapter explores one of the most important aspects of leadership — and that is the work that leaders do with and for themselves.

ENRICHMENT AND SELF-KNOWLEDGE

Generating self-knowledge and conducting ongoing work with your self/spirit.

- Knowing who you are and what makes you tick - self awareness.

- Performing with integrity, maintaining personal values.

- Listening to your inner voice, intuition.

- Being open, having self-confidence and trusting in your own abilities.

- Taking risks, trying innovative approaches, being confident and decisive.

- Creating balance in your life.

- Maintaining self through contemplation, reflection and introspection.

The Young Man and his Lesson

I was only 22 years old when I moved to the big city to work in a large teaching hospital. I knew I would learn a great deal and the experience would prepare me in the best fashion for a future in nursing. Little did I know it would change the course of my life. After working on a medical-surgical floor I transferred to a medical-intensive care unit. As the nurse in charge of the unit one particular night, I entered the unit before the start of the shift to get report. The unit was quiet that night and there was enough staff so that I could be the charge nurse and take just one patient who was soon to be admitted. Sometime after midnight, he arrived. He was a young man, perhaps in his mid-to late 20s. He was handsome, too, as I recall. I remember thinking to myself that it was going to be a good night in the intensive care unit. He only had one intravenous line, an unusual occurrence in the intensive care unit, and required little monitoring. I do not remember anything about his medical condition or what brought him to the unit, but I do remember vividly what happened that night.

Once I had checked him in, I set about to see that everyone else in the unit was doing well. I had time to accomplish a few charge nurse tasks and talk with my patient. He was a kind and gentle man, and he wanted to talk. We talked all night long, about many things but mostly about life. He told me to learn all that I could in my lifetime and that learning was part of the life journey. He said that I should seize opportunities as they came my way, as they might only come once. He was adamant about how important it was to tell people what I thought and felt, especially those I loved. He believed each day should be special and that everyone could find something special if they chose to look for it. He asked me to seek happiness and joy, not to wait for it to find me. Not only did he think I should stop to smell the roses, but that I should see beauty even in the weeds. He told me that life was short and very special, and that I should not waste a minute of it, as it would slip away quickly. It seemed that the entire night was dedicated to teaching me.

The morning was approaching. As in most intensive care units, there was little natural light, and this unit had only a few small, thin windows. From his bed he could see through one, and together we watched the dark sky turn light and the sun rising, until it burst upon the new day. Shortly after that he stopped breathing. The emergency call was made and the resuscitation team descended upon us. I do not remember what I did, what was done, or how it happened. What I do remember is that he died, right then, at the start of that new day.

I will never forget that young man. I will never forget what he taught me. While it was many years later that I truly realized his gift, I have tried to live as he told me to live. As he suggested, I seized opportunities as they arose, so that I might never look back and wonder, what if? What I learned then and continue to learn is that it is up to me. I choose to listen, to learn, to grow, to have control in my life and to see life as a wonderful journey. I try to make a difference for others...just as he made a difference for me.

Leadership abilities are enhanced by self-knowledge, and they become increasingly developed the more one knows about themselves-one's own values, beliefs and what matters in life. The more certain leaders are about their own principles, values, and motivations, the easier it is to stay consistent and confident in the day-to-day work as a leader. This self-relationship is also pertinent to the relationships leaders develop with those they lead. Leadership development, like self-development involves an ongoing commitment to learning and in essence are one in the same.

Knowing Who You Are

There is no information about the development of self or the importance of self-knowledge for leaders in the long-term care literature. Self-knowledge is the process of learning about the self, the inner being, soul, or spirit. It is the process of learning who you are, what you think, believe and value. Leaders need to have a solid sense of self. They can't lead others if they don't know who they are, what they want, or where they are going.

This theme, enrichment and self-knowledge, should actually be first in the model because this knowledge is critical for leadership. However, this concept seems to be the most threatening and frightening subject to many leaders, CEOs and administrators. Afraid or unaware, they occupy themselves with tasks to fill their days, never slowing down long enough to think or reflect. It is difficult to lead, to vision, or to dream, when consumed by the day-to-day problems and crises, uncertain what direction to take and frightened by what is yet to come.

If leaders are unaware of who they are, where they are headed and what matters to them in life and work, there will be no consistency in the way they lead or decisions they make. Their actions will be thoughtless reactions, taking on only the events of the moment. They may make different decisions given the same scenario. This constant change and inconsistency makes it hard for their coworkers to know what they want and how the leader wants them to behave. No one can follow because they do not know what direction the leader will take today or tomorrow. The leaders and the organization will be pulled in one direction or the other, determined by the crisis of the moment.

The desire to increase one's self-awareness, and the search for what one deems important in life comes to people in various ways at different times.

Many people get to a point in their life when they start to reflect on the meaning of their existence. It often happens in mid life, earlier for some, and later for others. Sometimes it happens as a result of a tragedy - the loss of a friend, or family member. It is often the response to a major change in life, such as a loss of a job, death of a loved one, a divorce or an illness.

Others may come to this point in their lives by enrolling in a class on self-development, personal growth or leadership, or questioning those qualities. Others may simply seek growth through self-initiation. Some people never get to this point in their lives, or at least never allow themselves to be conscious of it.

Performing with Integrity and Personal Values

Leaders must be consistent about their actions, values and person, day in and day out. When they are clear about their own direction, those around them know what to do and what to expect. A leader's decisions will be consistently driven by what the leader thinks and values. Given that consistency, those who follow will be able to make decisions that the leader would make without consultation. It will free up time for the leader while keeping the organizational values and vision intact.

Leaders who are in touch with their inner soul are certain of their values and beliefs and are confident in themselves and their abilities. Part of this self-development is to identify one's personal values and principles and to live them every day. When people compromise their values, it breaks them apart, as their actions do not speak for their beliefs, values, for their soul. Integrity is when one's actions are consistent with one's values, all the time, in all circumstances. When acting with integrity, the decision may not be easy, but a knowledgeable leader is certain and decisive. Questioning a decision and feeling uneasy about it is an indication of not remaining consistent with one's values.

Leaders need to do personal work making decisions that they know are right and not doing things that conflict with their principles — even if that means saying no to others. If leaders do what they know is not right, ethically or morally, they will lose respect for themselves and find it difficult to respect others.

Listening to Inner Voice and Intuition

Intuition is a feeling, a knowing without the use of data or exhaustive analysis. Often referred to as a "gut reaction," an intuitive feeling is strong and often right. One just needs to be aware and in touch with those feelings. Intuitive skills, in fact, can be learned and developed.

Many people seem so afraid of being quiet and still, reluctant to stop the frenzied pace. But there is great value in taking time to be quiet and listen. When the mind is quiet, answers come, solutions appear, and the self awakens. What is truly important comes from within. The happiness and joy everyone seeks comes from being in touch with their inner nature/self and not from the items and things accumulated on the outside.

Being Open and Trusting One's Abilities

Leaders trust others because they have come to know and trust in themselves. Trust and confidence nurture the ability to be innovative, creative and risky and to travel where others have not gone. This self-assurance enhances one's ability to make decisions because of a certainty about values and goals. Being confident and secure in one's self allows leaders to celebrate and recognize the contributions of others, giving credit to others and not needing it for the self. Maintaining self-awareness takes time, time for silence, contemplation, reflection, study and new learning. It is a life-long journey of growth, learning and evolving as a human being and as a leader.

Leaders who are open-minded will find new ways of thinking about things, accomplishing tasks, and dealing with issues. They will examine new programs, visit other facilities, seek out those who are successful, or talk to the experts. They might find a coach or a mentor and learn from them; they do not have to re-invent the wheel. Leaders create their own vision and progress even further, propelled by information learned from those who have traveled before.

Leaders need to be open to new learning, even when the situation is a negative one, or one with a negative outcome. Sometimes things do not always turn out right, but leaders must learn from those situations too. Learning from mistakes and failures is sometimes the very best learning. If leaders are not open to learning from mistakes, they are destined to repeat them.   Sometimes what appears to be a negative outcome or a failure is a sign to move in another direction, or to pursue another path.   Leaders need to embrace the hard times as well, as it is all a part of the learning and the journey.

Courage to be Innovative and Decisive

Leaders with self-knowledge control what happens to them in their work. While outside forces may push or pull them, these leaders decide how they are going to handle these forces.   If nothing more, leaders have the choice about how they feel about it.   An administrator may encounter a regulation or corporate mandate that is perceived as silly and ineffective.   They have a choice about whether to follow it or not, whether to try to fight it, or how to work around it so that it has little negative effect on the facility.   Leaders control their actions and attitude.

Self-knowledge enhances confidence and provides direction, as leaders are no longer satisfied with being pushed around by chance or circumstances in life.   They gain the power to decide and set a direction by being self-assured, confident, courageous and willing to try new things, to change.   Self-exploration and connection are not frightening, but exciting.   They create a new awareness - the beginning of a wonderful journey that can change one's life.

Leaders who are in touch with who they are, what they want and a willingness to do whatever it takes to get where they want to go will succeed. Confident in whom they are and what they want to accomplish, they seek to be the best, not settling on less for themselves or those they lead.   While maintaining their values, they are willing to take risks, to try new things and change.   Leaders are not afraid of the consequences, they are confident in their decisions.

As a result, such leaders are more innovative and willing to try new things, going where others have not.   They are willing to travel on a different path, as it makes sense and they are doing what they know is right, all in the service to others.   Just because it has been done one way in the past does not stop them if they think that there is a better way to go.

Creating Balance

Taking care of the self involves balance. In order to be a whole individual, and to make the right decisions for self and others, it is necessary to value all aspects of life, including work, family, and spirit. While many unbalanced, workaholic leaders have been financially successful, I believe that they have paid a very high price. The price is that of the self and of connections to friends and family. At some point in their lives, I believe those workaholics will look back and wish that they had chosen a more balanced life.

In later life and often in times of crisis, people reflect on what they would have done differently. Often people get to the end of their life only to realize that they have lived a shallow and unbalanced life, focused on work and tasks. Many wish they had led a more balanced life, spending more time with family and friends, doing more of life's pleasurable things.

While there will be times in life when work requires much of the leader's time, leaders need to learn to evaluate when they truly need to be the one doing the task or when whatever keeps them at work can be done by another or at a later time. Some administrators find it difficult to delegate responsibilities to other staff members, even those who are prepared to step in and carry the load. However, if other people are never prepared for appropriate tasks, the organization will grow past the point where the administrator controls all and does all. It is stifling. It also indicates to others that you do not trust them to do things well, which is demoralizing to your managers and other staff.

Leaders must prepare staff and then delegate. Staff will not always accomplish a task or job well or correctly. This becomes an opportunity for teaching. Keep giving the project back with directions until it is completed appropriately. Once learned, it relieves the leader of time pressures and they can focus on other tasks.

Maintaining Self through Reflection and Introspection

It is important to spend time daily in quiet reflection. People do this in a variety of ways. Some find the best opportunity is to think quietly when they walk, jog or exercise. Driving in silence, meditating and praying are other ways of accomplishing this task. Whatever the method, the day must involve time to think.   Establishing routine times for reflection serves to accomplish this important task.

With all of the issues at work, few people have enough time to do all that they want to do in a day.   However, in this one area, leaders need to be selfish. It will help enable them to travel in a better direction, with more solutions to problems, enhanced creativity and peace. As such the leader will be more aware, conscious of direction, confident in decisions and productive.

In order to give to others, leaders need to fill themselves or they will have little left to give.   While there are always things that need to be done and the "in box" always has something in it, leaders must stop and take this time for self.   Doing so is critical in order to maintain the self and to stay in touch with what truly matters.

It is never too late to start the process of learning about one's self, and growing in knowledge and fulfillment.   In a personal development seminar, a male participant stood up to announce to the group that he was 76 years old and just now discovering the man he was inside.   He was excited, elated with being in touch with his feelings and discovering what was truly important to him in his life.   This gentleman encouraged the group to continue searching, spending time in internal dialog with their hearts.   He asked the group to create a sense of urgency about this task, vowing not to wait another minute or they would be destined to look back as he did, wishing he had discovered what truly mattered to him many years before. Although he was 76 years old, he was celebrating, for at least in this lifetime he found it. Many don't.

FREQUENTLY ASKED QUESTIONS

Where do I possibly begin to do this self-exploration?

There are many books, workshops and seminars available. Seek them out and spend time with yourself in quiet reflection. Think about your work, family, life and person. Take time daily to think about your plans, future, interpersonal encounters and decisions, and how you feel about them. Be honest with yourself – you *know* how it feels inside.

We have always operated the same way. Why should I change now?

If it is working and all is fine, you may not need to make changes. But, for most of us, that is not the case. Many facilities have staff problems, census problems, survey concerns and financial concerns. Those who do not change may not survive.

I don't have any time now. How can I take any time out for myself?

Everyone has a full and busy life, but leaders manage to find time to do those things that are important to them. Time for you to think and plan is critical. If you do not have time to think, you are reacting to situations and issues, not acting in a logical, thoughtful way. In order to make good decisions, be creative, generate new ideas and programs, you need some time to be creative. You need time to fill yourself, to re-energize in order to be available to fulfill the needs of others.

CONCLUSION

John and Maria

John was an old-world craftsman and expert electrician with an 8th grade education who grew up with his family in Canada. Maria was one of nine children, a bright and determined woman who went through grade "13." They married August 12, 1939 and had two children.

They were a close family. After the children grew up and had families of their own, they often visited John and Maria in Michigan and looked forward to visits from their parents at their own homes in Ohio and Colorado. As John and Maria aged, the children noticed that Maria was losing her ability to cook, often forgetting how to make dishes that she had prepared a hundred times. Her inability to manage the home and conduct the simple daily tasks was evident. Maria would often leave notes around the house. One found by her daughter, Brenda read "John where are you I am in the kitchen." Brenda could see the stress it was putting on John.

In time Brenda convinced John and Maria to move to Ohio to be closer to her and her family. Maria had been diagnosed with Alzheimer's disease and John was finding it increasingly difficult to care for her without support. They moved to Ohio to live with his daughter in her home. Shortly after their arrival it became clear that this arrangement was not going to work.

Maria was up nearly every night wandering around the house. During the day she was confused, anxious and difficult to direct. The last straw occurred on a cold and snowy night when Brenda found Maria outside in the snow in only her nightgown. The family looked for a facility for Maria, found one and moved her there. John visited but continued living with his daughter. Over the next several weeks Maria adjusted and was doing well, but John was not. On several occasions, John did not remember conversations and repeated the same things over and over. This unusual behavior led Brenda to have him evaluated, and she found that he, too, was suffering with dementia, and he decided to move into the facility, as well.

In the beginning, though in different stages of the disease process, John and Maria were able to live together in the same room. In fact, the staff connected two of the" regulated" hospital beds together so that they might sleep in the same bed. When John could no longer cope with Maria's confusion or when he needed a rest, the staff would take her to another section of the facility and occupy her in activities to allow John some time alone. John also enjoyed going out of the facility on trips with other residents and visiting with his daughter at her home.

One night Maria suffered a heart attack and did not survive. John took her death hard, and in the coming months, he suffered from depression. He responded well to medication and spent time with his daughter and her family, sometimes spending the night or an entire weekend. But he missed Maria. Several months later John became quite ill and upon hospitalization was found to have had a stroke and colon cancer. In the hospital he talked of going home, and his daughter said that John indicated that "home" was the facility. Back at the facility, the staff spoiled him, worked hard to make him comfortable and to encourage him to eat. He had lost his appetite and would eat only a few bites and no more. Everyone tried to get him to eat; all staff in every department. They brought homemade dishes and desserts, to no avail. While not outwardly affectionate before, John would thank everyone individually, and often offer a kiss on the cheek. John knew. The staff knew. John wanted to be with Maria.

On a Saturday in August, the administrator received a call from the staff that John was not doing well. The administrator went to the facility, but John had died by the time she arrived. Brenda had been visiting all morning, but had left to pick up one of her children and wasn't there when John died. A short while later, the administrator met Brenda at the door, and while she knew her father's death was imminent, she took it poorly. After all, she had lost her mother a few years before. Staff was in and out of his room as she sat with him, comforting one another. As she was leaving later in the day, she said that she had just realized that the date was August 12th - her parent's 61st wedding anniversary. John, she believed, did not want to celebrate another wedding anniversary without Maria.

After the funeral service, Brenda told the staff that she put a few things he had received from the facility in the casket with him, including some photos taken there. She also put in "two red shirts." She said that the shirts had hung in his closet for years and he had refused to throw them out, even though their style was out of date and they did not fit well. John insisted on keeping them and told her when Maria was in the early stages of Alzheimer's disease, she always wanted John to wear one of his two red shirts any time that they left the house. Maria believed that if John was in his red shirt, she could always find him. The red shirt brought great comfort to Maria. Brenda put the red shirts in the casket with John so that Maria could find him.

Staff who work in long-term care are like the red shirts. Residents look for us, seek to find us, to keep them in touch, whole and connected. They look to us for comfort, reassurance, and peace. They look for us to alleviate the feelings of being lost, and replace it with the feelings of exhilaration at being found. We become the red shirts in their lives.

Purpose of the Book

The idea for this book originated with the desire to improve care and the environment for the residents and staff who live and work in long-term care. This book is one way of instituting concepts that may enhance the experience for all touched by a long-term care facility. Residents in long-term care deserve to live their final days in a happy, loving, caring and nurturing environment. Staff should have respectful, inclusive, open and caring environments in which to work.

In an effort to provide quality care to residents, the staff must be respected and cared for. Staff members who dedicate themselves to working in long-term care in all departments deserve more money than they currently earn. Most of all, they deserve respect and dignity. They should be elevated – not looked down upon. Warm, kind and compassionate, they give much of themselves to their work. But, they need administrators and health care professionals who care about them, too. When leaders care about the followers, employees will not only follow but will exceed expectations.

The purpose of this book is to share a leadership model and experience. The model was developed as a result of numerous years of experience in long-term care, the experience of one facility in which model components were used. It was also grounded in an extensive review of the leadership literature and years of experience as an administrator observing and studying the industry. The project was not developed using an existing leadership model or a particular theory. A few individuals who shared the same values, beliefs and vision designed this project. They in turn, solicited others who could share in the vision and who were interested in building programs and a project with service at the heart of the design. It was an evolutionary process.

The model and the mechanisms for implementation covered in this book serve as a guide for others interested in developing caring and nurturing cultures in long-term care. It is presented to encourage those on the path to creating service-oriented environments to improve the quality of life for long-term care residents and staff who work with them. Administrators may take some component or the entire model and implement what is appropriate for their particular setting. Each administrator will chart his or her own course.

This book is intended to encourage thought, generate discussion and promote research into the effects of organizational leadership in long-term care. It is also to bring the administrator to the forefront in determining the direction for long-term care and to encourage their involvement with other professionals in the field.

The Model

This is an examination of a leadership model that was effective in the development of a facility. Every leader needs to find his or her style and way of doing things. This is an opportunity to look at one model and how that model was implemented. Some organizations will embrace some of the model; others will use all of it in their organization. Many administrators already utilize some of the strategies described here and have created successful environments for residents, staff and families. The point is to take this model and develop and implement programs that fit each situation, specific needs and each facility. This book has presented concepts and ideas to consider. Model components serve as a starting point. Leaders must think about the seven basic themes and develop their own path.

Everyone is looking for "the answer," "the program," or "the solution." It is not that simple. If it were just one issue, the industry would have solved the problem a long time ago. Success involves an entire organization, a total system, and it takes leaders.

This specific model has not been put to the test through research. However, this leadership model in one facility has generated many positive outcomes. It has experienced a satisfied and content staff over the past 18 years, demonstrated by positive ratings on staff surveys, job longevity, lack of a need to ever utilize staffing agencies, multiple local and national staff and facility awards, teamwork, and in the acts of generosity, love and kindness shown by staff each day.   Inspections and state surveys have been positive and some years yielding perfect performance with no deficiencies or citations.   For families, the model has served to provide care that brought a number of letters from families about exemplary staff and care.   The facility census has been maintained and the reputation in the community is excellent.   The facility has also been recognized several times in commendations from the state legislature, letters and comments from visitors, including other professionals, and serves as a setting for local, national and international visitors.

Hope for the Use of this Book

I have spent a great deal of time with administrators in meetings and seminars.   When I visit their facilities, I note their actions and behaviors. When my colleagues spoke, I listened with interest as they shared their thoughts, feelings, beliefs, values and frustrations.   People working in the long-term care industry were willing to talk with me as a member of the industry and colleague. They openly shared their fears and frustrations, their successes and failures and their dreams.   These interactions and observations have been painful and disturbing, yet valuable and enlightening.   What I have learned is that many administrators and leaders in long-term care deeply want to enhance care and the work experience – but they don't know how to do it…   Administrators would like to create a more pleasant, productive and fun environment, but do not know where to seek help or how to begin.

My experience from a research and consulting perspective is that many administrators are familiar with the words and concepts of excellent leadership but are unable to put them into practice on a day to day basis in a facility.   Thus the hope for this book is also to assist and teach administrators in training and in practice how to turn these concepts into realities of daily life in a facility.

It is hoped that this book will generate interest and discussion about the role of the administrator as leader in long-term care.   It is important to raise the level of awareness about the impact that administrators can have in the transformation of the long-term care culture.   Administrators are truly the ones with the ability to institute massive change and restructuring.

Leadership in long-term care never ends.   It is a role that needs attention forever.   The amount of time and involvement will vary but the need will always exist.   The amount of time and personal involvement demanded of a leader in starting a new project or job is intense.   It is also intense when changes occur or during a crisis.   Once a project or significant change is initiated and incorporated operationally, the investment of energy decreases. In addition, the amount of attention and time will lessen as administrators select the right people, train them, trust them, and then monitor progress.

The time for change is now.   Increasing numbers of elderly adults with fewer available caregivers will emerge in the next decade, and the numbers are predicted to grow.   It will take time, and there is little time left to make the sweeping changes required.   Many people from all walks of life will find themselves or a loved one in long-term care someday.   It is time to make living and working in a long-term care facility an experience we would want for ourselves and those we love.

SUGGESTED READINGS

Anniston, Michael, H. & Willford, Dan S. (1998). Trust Matters: New Directions in Healthcare Leadership. San Francisco: Jossey-Bass Publishers.

Autry, James. A. (1991). Love and Profit: The Art of Caring Leadership. New York: Avon Books, Inc.

Axelrod, Alan. (2000). Elizabeth I CEO: Strategic Lessons from the Leader Who Built an Empire. Paramus, NJ: Prentice Hall Press.

Bennis, Warren. (1997). Leaders: Strategies for Taking Charge. New York: Harper Collins Publishing Inc.

Bennis, Warren (1999). Managing People is Like Herding Cats. Provo: Executive Excellence Publications.

Blanchard, Kenneth (1999). Heart of a Leader. Escondido, CA: Ken Blanchard Company.

Bolman, Lee. G. & Deal, Terrence. E. (1995). Leading with Soul: An Uncommon Journey of Spirit. San Francisco: Jossey-Bass Publishers.

Bradley, Maryjane G. & Thompson, Nancy R. (2000). Quality Management Integration in Long-Term Care: Guideline for Excellence. Baltimore: Health Professions Press.

Buckingham, Marcus, & Coffman, Curt. (1999). First Break All The Rules: What The World's Greatest Leaders Do Differently. New York: Simon and Schuster.

Buckingham, Marcus. (2005). The One Thing You Need to Know: About Great Managing, Great Leading, and Sustained Individual Success. New York: Free Press.

Chappell, Tom. (1993). The Soul of a Business: Managing for Profit and the Common Good. New York: Bantam Books.

Collins, Jim. (2001). Good to Great: Why Some Companies Make the Leap and Others Don't. New York: Harper Collins Publishing Inc.

Conger, Jay, A. (1992). Learning to Lead: The Art of Transforming Managers into Leaders. San Francisco: Jossey-Bass Publishers.

Conger, Jay, A. (1998). Winning 'Em Over: A New Model for Management in the Age of Persuasion. New York: Simon & Schuster.

Covey, Stephen. (1998). Servant Leadership from the Inside Out. Insights on Leadership: Service, Stewardship, Spirit and Servant Leadership (p xi-xvii). New York: John Wiley & Sons, Inc.

De Pree, Max. (1990). Leadership is an Art. New York: Dell Publishing.

De Pree, Max. (1992). Leadership Jazz: *The Art of Conducting Business Through Leadership, Followership, Teamwork, Touch, Voice.* New York: Dell Publishing.

Eckert, Lorie, K. (1997). Get Quiet and Listen. Gretna, LA: Pelican Publishing Company, Inc.

Goleman, Daniel. (1995). Emotional Intelligence: Why It Can Matter More Than IQ. New York: Bantam Books.

Goleman, Daniel, Boyatzis, Richard, McKee, Annie. (2002). Primal Leadership: Realizing the Power of Emotional Intelligence. Boston, MA: Harvard University Press.

Greenleaf, Robert. K. (1991). Servant Leadership: A Journey into the Nature of Legitimate Power and Greatness. Mahwah, NJ: Paulist Press.

Heerman, Barry. (1997). Building Team Spirit: Activities for Inspiring and Energizing Teams. New York: McGraw-Hill.

Helgesen, Sally. (1995). The Web of Inclusion: A New Architecture for Building Great Organizations. New York: Bantam Doubleday Dell Publishing Group, Inc.

Henry, L. G. & Henry, J. D. (1999). Reclaiming Soul in Health Care: Practical Strategies for Revitalizing Providers of Care. Chicago: Health Forum, Inc.

Jaworski, Joseph. (1996). Synchronicity: The Inner Path of Leadership. San Francisco: Berrett Koehler Publishers, Inc.

Johns, M. & Lawler, T. J. (1999). Leading Academic Health Centers. In Gilkey, R. W. (ed.) The 21st Century Health Care Leader. San Francisco: Jossey-Bass Publishers.

Jones, Laura Beth. (1995). Jesus CEO: Using Ancient Wisdom for Visionary Leadership. New York: Simon and Schuster, Inc.

Kane, Rosalie. A., Kane, Robert. L., & Ladd Richard. C. (1998). The Heart of Long-Term Care. New York: Oxford University Press.

Klein, Donald, C. (2001). New Vision, New Reality: A Guide to Unleashing Energy, Joy, and Creativity in Your Life. Center City, MN: Hazeldon.

Kohles, M. K., Baker, W. G., & Donaho, B. A. (1995). Transformational Leadership: Renewing Fundamental Values and Achieving New Relationships in Health Care. USA: American Hospital Publishing.

Kouzes, James. M., & Posner, Barry, Z. (1995). The Leadership Challenge: How to Keep Getting Extraordinary Things Done in Organizations. San Francisco: Jossey-Bass Inc. Publishers.

Kouzes, James. M., & Posner, Barry, Z. (1999). Encouraging The Heart: A Leader's Guide To Rewarding And Recognizing Others. San Francisco: Jossey Bass Inc. Publishers.

Kushner, Harold. S. (2001). Living a Life that Matters. New York: Random House.

Longest, Beaufort. B., Rakich, Jonathon. S., & Darr, Kurt. (2000). Management and Managers. In Managing Health Services Organizations and Systems, (4th ed). Baltimore: Health Professions Press.

Maxwell, John. (1993). Developing the Leader within You. Nashville: Thomas Nelson Publishers.

Porter-O'Grady, T. & Wilson, C. K. (1995). The Leadership Revolution in Health Care: Altering Systems, Changing Behaviors. Gaithersburg: Aspen Publishers, Inc.

Senge, Peter. M. (1994). The Fifth Discipline: The Art and Practice of the Learning Organization. New York: Bantam Doubleday Dell Publishing Group, Inc.

Thomas, William. H. (1996). Life Worth Living: How Someone You Love Can Still Enjoy Life in a Nursing Home. Acton, MA: Vanderwyk and Burnham.

Toms J.W., Toms, M. (1998). True Work: The Sacred Dimension of Earning a Living. New York: Bell Tower.

ABOUT THE AUTHOR

SUSAN D. GILSTER Ph.D. has a strong desire to improve the lives of individuals touched by our health care systems, the patients and families as well as the staff who work in health delivery environments. Susan has been involved in health care as a practitioner, manager, leader, developer, operator, educator and researcher for her entire career. Most of her time has been spent on health care project development and new and innovative initiatives. Her attraction to trying new strategies and programs and then to share the successes and failures has led to many years of publishing and presenting in meetings and conferences locally and around the world. Topics shared includes health care project development, leadership development, organizational change, Alzheimer's disease programs, staff satisfaction, recruitment and retention, family satisfaction, and environmental and behavioral interventions.

Most recently Dr. Gilster has been responsible for the development and operation of the Alois Alzheimer Center, the first freestanding Alzheimer's and dementia facility in the United States, which opened in May 1987. As Executive Director, she established a nationally recognized, specialized continuum of care for individuals with dementia. Under her direction the facility and staff have received numerous awards and recognitions including Step I National Quality Award from the American Health Care Association.

Dr. Gilster serves as an educational facilitator through affiliations with local and regional colleges and universities. She is a volunteer professor for the Colleges of Nursing and Health at The University of Cincinnati and Xavier University in Cincinnati as well as a preceptor to physicians, nurses and other health care related and management students in colleges and universities on a regional basis.

Susan's commitment to a making a contribution through research has led to her involvement in several research projects, from clinical interventions to experimental drug therapies. The unique work of the Alois Alzheimer Center has encouraged research nationally and internationally, as it has been a site for advanced degree student research. Many visitors involved in research and development have visited the Alois Alzheimer Center in an effort to encourage innovation in the field. Visitors from Japan, Holland, Australia, Mexico, Norway, Canada, are some of the countries representing a desire to improve health care.